THE HERMITAGE
in your pocket

D1540318

CONTENTS

THE HERMITAGE
in your pocket

Illustrated Guidebook

Alfa-Colour Art Publishers

Saint Petersburg, 2003

It is a well known fact that the Hermitage has everything: the gold of the Scythians and Ancient Greeks, Buddhist frescoes, Sassanian silver, Islamic bronze, treasures of the Great Moguls, Byzantine and Russian icons, Venetian lace... brilliant collections of European painting – Leonardo, Rembrandt, Poussin, Raphael, El Greco, Zurbaran, Cezanne, Matisse, Picasso... the creations of the jewellers Pauzié and Fabergé, Sèvres and Wedgwood services, English silverware and the works of Augsburg goldsmiths... then, finally, Manzu, Messina, Soutine, Kandinsky, Malevich...

The Hermitage is a whole constellation of remarkable architectural monuments: Rastrelli's Winter Palace, the chief residence of the Russian autocrats; Quarenghi's Hermitage Theatre; the New Hermitage, a masterpiece of museum construction by von Klenze and Stasov; Rossi's Triumphal Arch and the east wing of the General Staff, a superb adminstrative building by the same architect.

The Hermitage is a living monument to Russian history and culture. Its displays are housed in places where Russia's past is tangible: the room in which Peter the Great died; the apartments of Catherine II; the study where the last Empress wrote with a diamond on a window pane "Nicky is watching the hussars"; the White Dining-Room where the Provisional Government was arrested; the grand St George Hall where the first State Duma (parliament) was inaugurated; the Gallery of 1812 – a unique monument to Russia's victory over Napoleon.

The spirit of Russian history lives in the Hermitage's halls. The great masterpieces reveal more than just the thoughts and feelings of their creators: they remind us of how they

came to be in the museum, of Russia's cultural ties, of Russian cultural policy that was marked by especial openness to the whole world.

The Hermitage is a museum of world culture, created by the whole world and belonging to the whole world. Its doors open to welcome all those who love beauty, the labour and skill of talented hands – the fruits of artistic creativity.

The Hermitage is always pleased to make its visitors' encounter with it a happy one and this fact is borne out by the present guidebook *The Hermitage in your Pocket* — an aid and companion in delightful "wanderings" through the halls and displays of Russia's great museum.

Mikhail Piotrovsky
Director of the State Hermitage
Corresponding Member of the Russian Academy of Sciences
Corresponding Member of the Russian Academy of Arts
Professor of St Petersburg University
Doctor of Historical Sciences

The Hermitage is located at 34, Dvortsovaya Naberezhnaya (Palace Embankment) Entrance from the embankment and/or from Palace Square.

Transport: Metro stations *Gostiny Dvor* and *Nevsky Prospekt*. Bus 7 and trolleybuses 1, 7 and 10 from Nevsky Prospekt (get off at the stop after Palace Square).

Opening hours: Daily, except Monday, from 10.30 a.m. to 6.00 p.m. (5.00 p.m. on Sunday). Last entry one hour before closing.

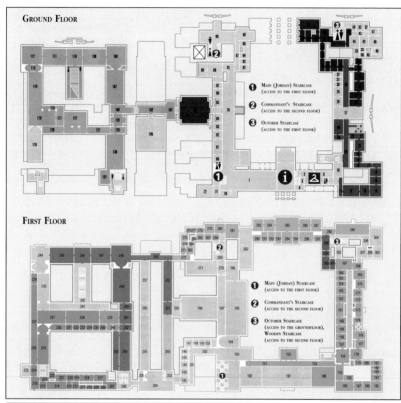

Information

The museum information desk **(i)** is situated in the main vestibule as you enter from the Neva embankment. There are computerized information stands that can give printed routes by the Main Staircase and opposite the foyer of the Hermitage Theatre.

Telephone information: +7 (812) 311 3420 and + 7 (812) 110 9625

Internet site: www.hermitagemuseum.org

Guided tours: Tours in Russian and foreign languages can be booked at the Excursion Office off the main vestibule. **Advance booking of tours by telephone:** +7 (812) 311 8446

Audio guides in Russian, English, French and German are available for hire in the main gallery, ground floor.

For less mobile visitors: Wheelchair hire. Apply to the information desk in the main vestibule or book in advance on +7 (812) 110 9079

Lecture hall: General Staff building, 45, Naberezhnaya Reki Moiki (Moika Embankment). Telephone: +7 (812) 110 9731.

Computer Educational Centre: Rastrelli Gallery, ground floor.

Schools Centre: Main Gallery, ground floor. Telephone: +7 (812) 110 9673

Youth Centre: General Staff building, 45, Naberezhnaya Reki Moiki (Moika Embankment). Telephone: +7 (812) 110 9530

Museum Shop: (books, postcards, copies of exhibits, souvenirs): Rastrelli Gallery, ground floor

Souvenir and Book stalls: Main gallery, ground floor; Main Staircase, upper landing; Main Staircase of the New Hermitage, upper landing; before the foyer of the Hermitage Theatre; in the Alexander Hall

Cafe: Rastrelli Gallery, ground floor

Internet Cafe: Rastrelli Gallery, ground floor

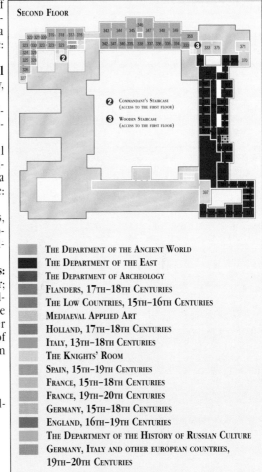

SECOND FLOOR

❷ COMMANDANT'S STAIRCASE (ACCESS TO THE FIRST FLOOR)

❸ WOODEN STAIRCASE (ACCESS TO THE FIRST FLOOR)

THE DEPARTMENT OF THE ANCIENT WORLD
THE DEPARTMENT OF THE EAST
THE DEPARTMENT OF ARCHEOLOGY
FLANDERS, 17TH–18TH CENTURIES
THE LOW COUNTRIES, 15TH–16TH CENTURIES
MEDIAEVAL APPLIED ART
HOLLAND, 17TH–18TH CENTURIES
ITALY, 13TH–18TH CENTURIES
THE KNIGHTS' ROOM
SPAIN, 15TH–19TH CENTURIES
FRANCE, 15TH–18TH CENTURIES
FRANCE, 19TH–20TH CENTURIES
GERMANY, 15TH–18TH CENTURIES
ENGLAND, 16TH–19TH CENTURIES
THE DEPARTMENT OF THE HISTORY OF RUSSIAN CULTURE
GERMANY, ITALY AND OTHER EUROPEAN COUNTRIES, 19TH–20TH CENTURIES

Branches of the Museum

The Winter Palace of Peter the Great
Memorial display devoted to Peter the Great in the private rooms of the Tsar's residence, reconstructed during restoration of the Hermitage Theatre. **Address:** 32, Dvortsovaya Naberezhnaya (Palace Embankment). Tickets are sold in the Hermitage ticket office in the Main Vestibule (34, Dvortsovaya Naberezhnaya). **Opening hours:** daily, except Monday, from 11.00 a.m. to 3.30 p.m. **Advance booking of guided tours:** +7 (812) 311 8446

Menshikov's Palace
The residence of the first governor of St Petersburg, constructed in 1710–11 on Vasilyevsky Island to the design of the architects Giovanni Fontana and Gottfried Schädel. **Address:** 15, Universitetskaya Naberezhnaya (University Embankment), Vasilyevsky Island. **Opening hours:** daily, except Monday, from 10.30 a.m. to 4.30 p.m. **Advance booking of guided tours:** +7 (812) 311 8446

The General Staff building
Address: 6/8, Dvortsovaya Ploshchad (Palace Square). **Opening hours:** daily, except Monday, from 10.30 a.m. to 6.00 p.m. (5.00 p.m. on Sunday). Last entry one hour before closing. **Advance booking of guided tours:** +7 (812) 311 8446

THE HERMITAGE
Past and Present

The Hermitage is one of the world's most famous museums. Its collections number over 2,700,000 items, spanning the whole history of world culture from the Stone Age to the twentieth century. Especially noted are the collections of Western European art, Scythian and Ancient Greek gold and the art of Antiquity and the East. Its stocks of furniture, silver, porcelain, arms and armour, carpets and fabrics are stunningly rich. The museum has six departments: Western European art, the Ancient World, archaeology, the East, the history of Russian culture and numismatics. Its displays occupy seven buildings. Five of them form St Petersburg's main architectural ensemble: the Winter Palace, Small, Old and New Hermitages and the Hermitage Theatre. The Hermitage also possesses the left wing of the General Staff building across Palace Square and the Menshikov Palace on Vasilyevsky Island.

The museum goes back over 200 years. The date of its foundation is usually taken to be the year 1764, when the first collection was acquired. Strictly speaking, its history began even earlier with the Winter Palace, the chief residence of the Russian tsars. The first Winter Palace in St Petersburg was built by the city's founder, Peter the Great (1682–1725). After Peter's death, his palace fell into disrepair and Empress Anna Ioannovna (1730–1740) occupied the nearby mansion of Admiral General Apraxin. This residence was too cramped and unattractive for Empress Elizabeth (1741–1761) and in

Johann Baptist Lampi the Elder
Portrait of Empress Catherine II
1793. Oil on canvas

1754 the architect Francesco Bartolomeo Rastrelli began a new Winter Palace, a magnificent product of the Russian Baroque. In December 1761 Elizabeth died without seeing the palace finished. Its first real owner was Catherine II (1762–1796), whose reign saw Russian culture flourish and gave us the Hermitage.

Catherine had the Winter Palace completed. Some of the finest architects worked on its decoration: Yury Velten and Ivan Starov from St Petersburg, the Frenchman Jean-Baptiste Vallin de la Mothe and the Italian Giacomo Quarenghi. The Empress gave orders for a "hermitage" — a place of seclusion — to be built alongside the palace. Such garden pavilions were used for gatherings of a close circle of friends. Since the Winter Palace had no garden, between 1764 and 1775 Velten and Vallin de la Mothe added a hanging garden at second-storey level. Pavilions were placed at its north and south ends. This complex later became known as the Small Hermitage. It was the Northern Pavilion that Catherine used for "dancing, games and dining" with the select few. The table was laid on the floor below and raised by a special mechanism, so as to avoid the presence of servants. This was also the place where the Empress's paintings and other art treasures were kept.

Her collection began more or less by chance. In 1764 Catherine agreed to accept in settlement of a debt owed by the Berlin merchant Gotzkowsky some pictures he had bought for Frederick the Great before the Prussian King had been bankrupted by war with Russia. Perhaps she wanted to rub a little salt in "Old Fritz's" wound, since in her youth her fate, as a minor German princess, had depended on him. Most importantly, though, the intelligent and ambitious Catherine grasped that the creation of an art gallery like those of European courts would raise her own prestige and the splendour of her reign, contributing to the image of an enlightened monarch to which she aspired. And Catherine devoted herself to collecting on a truly Russian scale. Sparing no expense, she bought up one major collection after another.

The Saxon minister Count Bruhl's six hundred paintings, purchased in 1769, laid the foundations of the collection of Dutch and Flemish painting. In 1779 that collection was expanded by the works of Rubens, Van Dyck and Snyders that came in as part of the collection of British prime-minister Robert Walpole. More than 1,000 drawings from the Bruhl collection, together with 4,000 acquired in Brussels a year earlier, from the collection of Count Cobenzl, provided the basis for the Hermitage's Department of Drawing,

View of the Neva from the Winter Palace roof

The Large Hall in the Northern Pavilion of the Small Hermitage. Drawing by Julius Friedenreich. 1840

one of the world's largest collections of graphic art.

Honestly admitting to understanding "nothing in either music or painting", Catherine was wise enough to employ the services of experts that were among the finest minds of the day: the diplomat Prince Dmitry Golitsyn, the philosopher-Encyclopaedists Diderot and Grimm and the sculptor Falconet. It is to their tastes, knowledge and energy that the Hermitage owes many of its masterpieces. In 1772, at the prompting of the Geneva-based collector Tronchin, supported by Golitsyn and Diderot, Catherine purchased one of the finest collections in Europe that had been assembled by the Parisian connoisseur Pierre Crozat — over 400 paintings, including celebrated "highlights" of the Hermitage, such as Giorgione's *Judith*, Rembrandt's *Danaë*, Rubens's *Bacchus* and *Lady-in-Waiting* and works by French painters. The Empress also collected cameos and intaglios with a passion she compared to a disease. In 1778 she acquired the superb cameo collection of the Duc d'Orléans, that became the foundation of the Hermitage's extremely rich stocks of Ancient and Western European glyptics. Catherine was less interested in sculpture. Nevertheless, in 1785 she purchased 200 sculptures from the British banker Lyde Browne (admittedly for the summer residence of Tsarskoye Selo). Later the gem of that collection — Michelangelo's *Crouching Boy* —became one of the Hermitage's precious assets. In the early 1780s the Parisian sculptor Jean-Antoine Houdon produced a marble statue of Voltaire for the Empress. Works commissioned from contemporary artists and purchases made in the studios of leading European figures were a further source for the stocks of Catherine's Hermitage. It also acted as the repository for items presented to the Empress, such as snuff-boxes, of which she was fond, that can now be seen in the Gallery of Jewellery. At the end of Catherine II's reign her Hermitage museum contained over 3,000 paintings, over 7,000 drawings, 80,000 prints, 10,000 engraved gems and more than 1,300 works of jewellery. It was one of the best collections in Europe.

The growing stocks required larger premises. In the late 1770s and 1780s, Velten linked the two pavilions of the Small Hermitage with galleries and constructed the Old Hermitage (as it

The Peacock Clock in the Eastern Gallery of the Small Hermitage. Watercolour by Konstantin Ukhtomsky. 1860s

was later called) further up the embankment. The collections were installed here and here Catherine relaxed or devoted herself to "scholarly pursuits" — reading, carving cameos and even scientific experiments. Additionally the building served to link the Winter Palace and Small Hermitage with the Hermitage Theatre. The theatre was one of Catherine's passions and an important element of court life. The Hermitage Theatre and adjoining Raphael Loggias block were constructed by Quarenghi in the 1780s. These were the last elements to be added to the complex in the eighteenth century and completed Catherine's Hermitage.

In the nineteenth century the Hermitage turned from a personal art collection and place of private relaxation into a public museum. The decisive event in this process was the erection of the last building of the Hermitage ensemble — the New Hermitage and the opening of the "Imperial Museum" within it. An impetus of a kind, purely external, was provided by the devastating fire in the Winter Palace in December 1837. Restored by 1839 under the guidance of the architect Vasily Stasov with the participation of his colleague Alexander Briullov, the Winter Palace emerged more brilliant than ever. This prompted the master of the Hermitage, Nicholas I (1825–1855), to refurbish the existing Hermitage buildings and create a separate building as a museum like those that were then appearing in Europe. A plan was commissioned from Leo von Klenze, the Bavarian architect who designed the Pinakothek in Munich. A romantic and expert on Ancient architecture, von Klenze conceived the "museum" along the lines of an ancient "dwelling of the muses". Constructed in 1839–51 by Stasov (who amended

Franz Krüger
Portrait of Emperor Nicholas I
1850s. Oil on canvas

*The entrance and Vestibule
of the New Hermitage.* Watercolour
by Konstantin Ukhtomsky. 1853

the design where necessary) and Nikolai Yefimov, the building was officially styled the New Hermitage. Linked by passageways to the Old and Small Hermitages and the Winter Palace beyond, the new Hermitage completed the ensemble we know today. On 6 February 1852 the Imperial Museum was formally inaugurated. The Hermitage welcomed its first visitors. At first public access to the museum was limited, but in the late 1860s the restrictions were lifted.

In the nineteenth century the Hermitage collections grew with less intensity but more purpose than in the eighteenth. The almost complete absence of Spanish and Old Netherlandish paintings was overcome, for example. The museum acquired a number of masterpieces. In 1865 Leonardo's *Litta Madonna* was purchased in Milan and in 1870 Alexander II (1855–1881) presented his wife Maria Alexandrovna with Raphael's *Conestabile Madonna*. The painting hung in the Empress's study in the Winter Palace together with others and came to the Hermitage after her death in 1880.

The main priority in the nineteenth century, however, was not the expansion of the Picture Gallery that was in any case regarded as exceptionally rich, but the creation of new sections, especially one devoted to the Ancient World section that Catherine's Hermitage had lacked: Nicholas I, keen to have a museum of European standard, bought up ancient sculpture and pottery, while encouraging archaeological researches in the south of Russia that provided the Hermitage with its celebrated collection of Graeco-Scythian antiquities. The real birth of the ancient department came, however, under Tsar Alexander II (1855–1881), in the year 1861 with the purchase in Rome of the Campana collection — some 100 statues and over 500 painted vases. By the turn of the twentieth century, in the last years of the Russian monarchy, the Hermitage was already a museum and research institution of European significance. Its crowned owners did not involve themselves in the life of the museum and new acquisitions practically ceased. The last notable addition to the Imperial Hermitage took place in 1914, in the reign of Nicholas II (1894–1917), with the purchase of Leonardo's *Madonna with a Flower*.

For the Hermitage the twentieth century really began with the revolutions in 1917. They put an end to the history of the Imperial Museum and began that of the State Hermitage. Immediately after the October Revo-

The Crimson Study
Watercolour by Luigi Premazzi. 1869

lution, the Hermitage started to receive nationalized private collections and palace treasures. They found a safe refuge in the museum and considerably enriched it. For example, the picture gallery that had gone no further than the eighteenth century in the Imperial Hermitage, was now extended chronologically as far as the early twentieth. First, in 1922, Nikolai Kushelev-Bezborodko's collection of paintings from the first half of the nineteenth century was transferred to the Hermitage from the Academy of Arts; then, in 1948, the museum gained paintings by the Post-Impressionists and French artists of the turn of the twentieth century from the Moscow collections of Sergei Shchukin and Ivan Morozov. (The Museum of New Western Art in Moscow, where they had been kept since the revolution, was disbanded and the paintings were threatened with destruction as they did not accord with official Soviet ideology. By dint of great efforts they were brought safely to the Hermitage, but had to wait until the late 1950s before they were shown to the public.)

The gathering in the Hermitage of an immense quantity of items from the Ancient World, the East and Russia led to the creation of new departments and sections: the Department of the East in 1920, Archaeology in 1931 and the History of Russian Culture in 1941. More buildings came under the museum's auspices and new displays were set up: an exhibition on the culture of Peter the Great's time opened in the Menshikov Palace in 1966; Peter's personal rooms in his

**Panorama
of Palace Square
and the General Staff building**

Winter Palace were reconstructed during the restoration of the Hermitage Theatre in the late 1980s. In the 1990s, in the left wing of the General Staff building (constructed by Carlo Rossi in 1820–27), displays of Empire-period art and the decorative ensembles of Pierre Bonnard and Maurice Denis were installed.

In the twentieth century the Hermitage's stocks increased more than fourfold. Items came in through purchases made by the Expert Commission and, especially, from archaeological and collecting expeditions. The Hermitage was enriched by unique works of primitive culture, ancient and early Russian art. A valuable contribution to the Hermitage collections was made by gifts from Western artists and collectors. That is, for example, how the museum acquired an interesting range of twentieth-century Italian sculpture. And, as the twentieth century drew to a close, the Hermitage was able to return to the practice, spurned in the Soviet period, of purchasing works on the European art market: some of the regrettably numerous gaps in the stocks of twentieth-century art have now been filled with paintings by Soutine, Utrillo and Rouault.

The story was not only one of acquisitions, however. Between 1928 and 1933, on government orders, more than forty masterpieces were sold abroad. Titian's *Venus with a Mirror*, Raphael's *Alba Madonna* and Jan van Eyck's *Annunciation* are now in American museums. There was tragedy in the years of the Second World War — evacuation of the collections behind the Urals, the struggle with starvation and death in besieged Leningrad. Through the heroic efforts of the staff, the Hermitage buildings, halls and collections were saved, the displays restored and the museum returned to productive life.

The Hermitage entered the twenty-first century in a state of energetic renewal and development. Its collections are growing. The event of the year 2002 was the acquisition of one of Malevich's variants of his famous *Black Square*. Interiors are being restored, new displays are being opened, the traditions of palace festivities and ceremonies are being revived and music can be heard in the halls that hospitably welcome the whole world.

THE WINTER PALACE

The Great Suite of State Rooms

The Great Suite of State Rooms is the heart of the Winter Palace. The succession of five halls running from the Main Staircase (1) to the Great Throne Room (198) was the setting for the most important ceremonies held in the imperial residence: Their Majesties' "entries", receptions of delegations and ambassadors, the proclamation of acts of state. The suite formed gradually over the late eighteenth century and the early decades of the nineteenth. The original architect of the building intended the main receptions halls to be located along the Neva. Catherine II, however, dismissed Rastrelli when he had finished only the Main Staircase and the Great Church. For almost thirty years the Empress made do with a small throne room in her apartments. Only in the 1790s did Giacomo Quarenghi create the Great Throne Room for her, adding a new block in the middle of the east side of the palace incorporating a hall with a floor area of 800 square metres. It was approached through a hall built by Yury Velten in 1774–75 in place of a gallery dating from Rastrelli's time. In the nineteenth century sculptures of warriors bearing the coats-of-arms of Russian cities on banners and standards were installed here and it became known as the Armorial Hall. In 1826, immediately in front of the Large Throne Room, Carlo Rossi constructed the Gallery of 1812 (197). Finally, in 1833–34, Auguste Montferrand created two halls between these and the Main Staircase: the Field Marshals' Hall (193) and the Peter the Great Hall (194). The Great Suite of State Rooms was complete. However, the fire that raged through the palace in December 1837 destroyed the decoration of the state rooms. They were restored by the architect Vasily Stasov who directed all the restoration work in the palace. On the orders of Nicholas I, Stasov recreated the Main Staircase, Montferrand's two halls and the Gallery of 1812 in keeping with the original designs. On the other hand, he decorated the Large Throne Room and Armorial Hall in his own way. He managed to unite halls with different architecture through a single idea and decorative finish, creating a suite of state rooms in the imperial palace that affirmed the greatness and might of the Russian Empire.

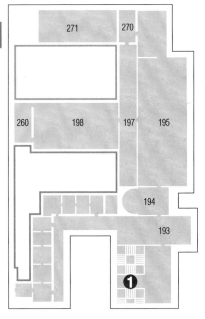

First Floor

❶ Main (Jordan) Staircase
(access to the groundfloor)

The Main Gallery. 1754–62; 1837–39
Architects: Francesco Bartolomeo Rastrelli; Vasily Stasov
This spacious gallery with three aisles whose vaults rest on mighty piers,
is decorated with sculpture and vases carved from light-coloured stone.
It leads from the vestibule of the Winter Palace to the Main Staircase.
The first steps can be seen from a long way off and in a niche a statue
of Power in a opulent Baroque setting greets every visitor to
the imperial palace.

The Main Staircase
1754–62; 1837–39
Architects: Francesco
Bartolomeo Rastrelli;
Vasily Stasov
In days gone by this was
known as the Jordan Staircase. During the Orthodox
feast of Epiphany in Janu-
ary a procession descend-
ed the staircase and went
out onto the frozen Neva,
where the ceremony of the
Blessing of the Waters took
place in memory of
Christ's baptism in the
Jordan.

The Main Staircase
Upper landing

Restored in the same Baroque style after the fire of 1837, the staircase is striking
for its luxurious grandeur and abundance of light. The stairwell occupies
the entire north-east part of the palace and rises to a height of some 22 metres.
The colourful ceiling painting depicting the gods on Olympus (by the eighteenth-century Venetian painter Diziani) creates the illusion of an opening
to the skies. The streams of light are reflected in numerous mirrors. Gilded mould-
ings – stylized plants, seashells and scrolls – frame the walls and windows and
ascend to the ceiling, giving the entire interior an air of gaiety, lightness and
brilliance. The white marble stairs ascend in two elegantly turned flights to an
upper landing that its crowned by ten monolithic columns of grey Serdobol granite with gilded bases and capitals. Everywhere we find marble and alabaster sculpture by Italian and Russian craftsmen of the eighteenth and nineteenth centuries – statues of ancient deities and muses, allegories affirming and glorifying
the might and wisdom of the country's rulers.

The Great Coronation Carriage. 1720s. Paris, France
Wood, metal, glass, leather, silk, cloth; carved, cast, gilded, embroidered and painted. Length 700 cm. (Hall 193)
Acquired by Peter the Great in Paris in 1717, this carriage may have been used for the coronation of Catherine II in 1763.

The Field Marshals' Hall
1833; 1838–39. Architects:
Auguste Montferrand;
Vasily Stasov. (Hall 193)
Austere architecture in a
strict Classical style, military motifs in the decorative painting and moulding
and bronze chandeliers
featuring depictions of
arms and armour, as well as
the portraits of Russian
field marshals that at one
time graced the walls of
this hall and gave it its
name – all this served as a
reminder of Russia's mar-
tial glory. The hall was used
for the ceremony of the
mounting of the guard performed by officers of the
Imperial Guards regiments.

The Hall of Peter the Great
1833; 1838–39
Architects: Auguste Montferrand;
Vasily Stasov. (Hall 194)

The hall that Montferrand created in memory of the first Russian emperor, Peter the Great, was recreated almost unchanged by Stasov after the fire. The walls here are lined with scarlet Lyons velvet with bronze Russian coats-or-arms and Peter's monograms – made from the first letters of *Petrus Primus* (Peter the First in Latin). The same motifs are repeated everywhere: at the base of the walls, in the moulding and murals. The paintings on the side walls – *The Battle of Poltava* and *The Battle of Lesnaya* by Barnaba Medici and Pietro Scotti – are reminders of Peter's greatest victories in the war with Sweden. A semicircular niche like the sanctuary of an Orthodox church, framed by a richly ornamented cornice and two columns of banded green jasper, contains Jacopo Amiconi's painting of Peter together with Minerva the goddess of wisdom and war. In front of the painting is a throne created by the court furniture-maker Meyer for Paul I in 1797, a copy of the throne in the Large Throne Room. Silver chandeliers, tables, candelabra and wall-lights together with a parquet floor of precious woods complete the sumptuous decor of this hall.

Jacopo Amiconi. 1675–1752
Peter the Great with the Goddess of Wisdom Minerva
Between 1732 and 1735. Oil on canvas. 231x178 cm

This allegorical painting depicting Peter the Great with Minerva, the Ancient Roman goddess of wisdom and war, was intended to glorify the Emperor's genius as a statesman and warrior. The canvas was painted by the Italian Amiconi in London to a commission from Prince Antioch Cantemir (1708–1744), Russia's ambassador to Britain who was also a satirical poet and one of the most educated men of his time. He was the son of the Moldavian hospodar Demetrius Cantemir, an ally and supporter of Peter the Great, and commissioned this painting as a token of his profound respect for the Emperor. Amiconi produced his work when Peter was already dead and, it is believed, used the portrait of Peter the Great that had been painted from life by the Frenchman Louis Caravaque, who worked in Russia in the Emperor's reign. Amiconi's painting was kept in the Winter Palace even before it was installed in this hall.

The Armorial Hall. 1838–39
Architect: Vasily Stasov. (Hall 195)

Claude Ballin. 1661–1754
Plât de Ménage table ornament. 1724–27
Paris, France. Cast, chased and engraved silver. Height 30 cm. (Hall 195)
This Rococo table ornament made up of a fruit-bowl on a base surrounded by candle-holders is the work of Louis XIV's outstanding medallist and jeweller Claude Ballin the Younger. This is one of the masterpieces of the extremely rich collection of eighteenth-century French silver, many items of which were commissioned by the Russian court and used in the Winter Palace.

The magnificent Corinthian colonnade supporting the gallery gives this hall with a floor area of 1,000 square metres a grand appearance. In the corners of the end walls there are sculptural groups of early Russian warriors. The bronze chandeliers carry shields bearing the coats-of-arms of the Russian provinces. This hall was used for receiving delegations from the provincial nobility or the cities of the Empire. During the Second World War it was hit by a shell that pierced the wall and floor near the entrance to the Peter the Great Hall. The hall was restored as magnificent as ever after the war and now houses a display of the Hermitage's very rich collection of Western European silverware.

George Dawe. 1781–1829. *Portrait of Prince Nikolai Rayevsky.* Circa 1825 Oil on canvas. 70 x 62.5 cm. (Hall 197) The valorous commander of an infantry corps, Nikolai Rayevsky (1771–1829) was also famous for the fact that he took his young sons with him to the Battle of Borodino, setting an example of courage for his soldiers.

The Gallery of 1812. 1826; 1838–39 Architects: Carlo Rossi; Vasily Stasov (Hall 197) This gallery was created in commemoration of Russia's victory over Napoleon. Its walls bear 332 portraits of Russian generals who participated in the campaigns of 1812–15. They were created in the years 1819–28 by the English artist George Dawe (1781–1829). During the fire the portraits were saved and the gallery was restored with little change to its original appearance.

George Dawe. 1781–1829 *Portrait of Prince Piotr Bagration* Circa 1823. Oil on canvas 70 x 62.5 cm. (Hall 197) Piotr Bagration (1758–1812, an infantry general and gifted military commander, was the descendant of a Georgian princely dynasty. He died of wounds received at Borodino and this portrait was painted from a now-unknown likeness produced in his lifetime.

George Dawe. 1781–1829 *Portrait of Prince Mikhail Kutuzov.* 1829 Oil on canvas. 361 x 268 cm. (Hall 197) Field Marshal Kutuzov, the commander in chief of the Russian army and architect of the victory over Napoleon, is depicted beneath a canopy of snow-laden pines with a panoramic view of a great battle in the background.

25

The Large Throne Room (St George Hall)
1838–41. Architect: Vasily Stasov. (Hall 198)
This hall, the main state room in the Winter
Palace, is one of Stasov's finest creations.
While retaining the layout and dimensions
of Quarenghi's Throne Room, Stasov decorated the room in the austere forms of nineteenth-century Russian Classicism, using
two expensive materials that combine very
effectively: white Carrara marble on the
walls and columns and chased and gilded
bronze, used for the bases and capitals of
the columns, the balustrade of the balcony
and applied ornament on the ceiling. The
complex pattern on the ceiling is a mirror-
image of the splendid parquet floor, made
from sixteen varieties of precious wood. The
throne dais stands beneath a relief image of
St George, the patron saint of Russian warriors and the imperial family. At the top of
seven velvet-covered steps the throne
stands beneath a canopy with a panel of the
coat-of-arms of the Russian Empire behind.
Nicholas Clausen created the throne in England in 1737 for Empress Anna Ioannovna.
It is made of wood mounted with gilded
silver and upholstered in red velvet embroidered with a double-headed eagle.

The Large Throne Room
The throne dais

The Great Church of the Winter Palace
1754–62; 1838–39
Architects: Francesco Bartolomeo
Rastrelli; Vasily Stasov. (Halls 270, 271)
Immediately adjoining the great suite
of state rooms is the Great Church:
grand Orthodox services were an important part of all the official ceremonies that took place in the imperial residence. This is one of the few
interiors in the palace that Rastrelli
managed to finish.

After the fire of 1837 Stasov restored the
church in keeping with Rastrelli's original
designs, retaining its sumptuous Baroque
appearance. The artists Fiodor Bruni and
Piotr Basin recreated the work of the Italian eighteenth-century painter Francesco
Fontebasso that had perished in the fire:
a *Resurrection* on the ceiling and figures
of the evangelists below. The church was
consecrated to the Resurrection in 1762,
but a year later, after Rastrelli's dismissal,
Catherine II had the church rededicated
to the Vernicle (a miraculous image of
Christ). Today the church is used for temporary exhibitions of icon-painting and
works of Christian art.

France, 15th–18th Centuries

Department of Western European Art

The display of French art of the fifteenth to eighteenth centuries occupies 25 halls in the second storey of the Winter Palace, running alongside Palace Square. In the eighteenth century this was the location of the apartments of Catherine II (Halls 271–281) and her son and heir, the future Paul I (Halls 283–297). After the fire of 1837 these two sets of apartments, redecorated by the architect Alexander Briullov, were kept in reserve. In the late 1920s they were turned into museum halls.

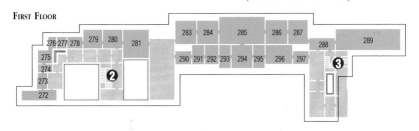

FRANCE, 15TH–18TH CENTURIES

② COMMANDANT'S STAIRCASE
(ACCESS TO THE SECOND FLOOR)

❸ OCTOBER STAIRCASE (ACCESS TO THE GROUNDFLOOR), WOODEN STAIRCASE
(ACCESS TO THE SECOND FLOOR)

FIRST FLOOR

The collection of French art of the fifteenth to eighteenth centuries is one of the largest in the Hermitage and, indeed, in the world, the second richest and most significant after the Louvre in Paris. The display includes sections devoted to the French Renaissance (Halls 272–274), represented chiefly by items of applied art; the seventeenth century (Halls 275–281) with masterpieces by the greatest artists of "the Age of Classicism"; and the eighteenth century (Halls 283–289) that is reflected in the Hermitage in all its fullness. The extremely rich collection of French applied art from the seventeenth and eighteenth centuries — furniture, tapestries, fabrics and embroidery, pottery, porcelain and bronzes — is displayed separately (Halls 290–297, overlooking the courtyard). The richness and value of the Hermitage's collection of old French art is the result of close cultural and artistic ties between Russia and France in the eighteenth century, during the reign of Catherine II. It was then that the core of the French collection in the imperial Hermitage was created as well as the private collections of the nobility that were nationalized after the revolution and considerably enlarged the museum's stocks.

France, 15th–18th Centuries

The Adoration of the Magi
Central part of a triptych
Early 16th century
The "High Brow" workshop, Limoges, France
Painted enamel on copper
Dimensions: 28 x 38.8 cm
(Hall 272)
Limoges was known as a centre producing articles decorated with enamel. Coloured glass-like compounds were applied to the surface of a copper plate and then fired in a kiln to produce beautiful, long-lasting compositions. In the early sixteenth century the technique of painted enamel established itself at Limoges, making it possible to achieve a natural-looking image. In this Gospel scene that was the central part of a portable altar we can easily recognize real figures, costumes and architecture characteristic of the Renaissance period.

Plate with a depiction of the myth of Psyche
Mid-16th century
Workshop of Pierre Reymond, Limoges, France
Technique. Dimensions:
(Hall 272)
In the middle of the sixteenth century, in the heyday of secular Renaissance culture in France, a "new school" of enamelling emerged in Limoges, employing a monochromatic painting technique that gave a special sense of volume and sensual expressiveness to the images. Those were most often subjects from Ancient history and mythology that was then in vogue and adorned not church plate, but festive tableware.

Master of the Thuison Altarpiece
The Entry into Jerusalem
Second half of the 15th century
Oil on panel. 116.5 x 51.5 cm
(Hall 274)
This painting is a panel from the altar
in the Abbey of St Honoré at Thuison in
Picardy. The remaining seven panels are
in the Art Institute of Chicago. One of the
earliest works of French easel painting, this
work combines a reverent delight in the
beauty of the earthly world in all its detail,
something characteristic of painting in
the Low Countries from where this new art
came, with the refinement and exquisite-
ness that mark French taste and style.

Bernard Palissy (1510–1589)
Dish. Circa 1560. Lead-glazed earthenware
47.5 x 35 cm. (Hall 273)
The "French Leonardo da Vinci", as the
scholar and engineer Bernard Palissy has
been called, invented a special type of
pottery known as "rustic ware". The deep
blue glaze in combination with naturalis-
tic depictions of amphibians, fish and
plants make this dish an embodiment
of the living beauty of nature on earth.

Jacques Bellange (active between 1602 and 1617). *The Lamentation*. 1615–17 Oil on canvas. 115 x 175 cm (Hall 274) Bellange, a painter, engraver and palace decorator, worked at the court of the Dukes of Lorraine. The tragically gloomy atmosphere of his paintings is not only an echo of the alarms felt in the age in which the artist lived, a time when the Renaissance ideals came to crisis, but also the result of the influence of Caravaggio's work on him.

Corneille de Lyon (Early 16th century – 1575) *Female Portrait*. Mid-1530s Oil on panel. 20 x 15.5 cm (Hall 274) Corneille was one of the outstanding French portraitist of the Renaissance era. This portrait is of a lady of the court of King Francis I (1515–1547) whose reign saw Renaissance culture reach its height in France. This small work made exceptionally attractive by the exquisite, strict composition, the refined colour scheme and charming image.

The portrait was one of the most significant phenomena in French Renaissance art. National character and taste manifested themselves particularly vividly in it. The French sixteenth-century portraitists did not leave us many works. The splendid examples in the Hermitage collection are a great rarity and occupy a very prominent place in the display of French art.

Unknown 16th-Century Artist. *Portrait of the Duc d'Anjou(?)*. Second half of the 16th century
Oil on panel. 48.5 x 32 cm (Hall 274)
Expressive precision marks this image of a French aristocrat in whose face the artist has brought out the tense caution of a man living in an atmosphere of dangerous intrigues such as prevailed at the royal court during the age of religious wars in the late sixteenth century. This maybe a likeness of Henri de Valois who was destined to be the last king of France from that dynasty.

Pierre Dumoustier the Elder (Circa 1545–before 1610). *Portrait of a Youth*. Last third of the 16th century
Oil on canvas. 32 x 19 cm (Hall 274)
This is an extremely rare example of a portrait painted in oils by Pierre Dumoustier, a noted master of the pencil portrait. In both his drawings and this painting, the artist pursued subtle psychological characterization, revealing the depth and complexity of his subject's inner life, the mind hard at work, animating the youth's features.

Simon Vouet (1590–1649)
Allegorical Portrait of Anne of Austria. Circa 1643
Oil on canvas. 202 x 172 cm
(Hall 275)
Vouet, the head of the court school in the first half of the seventeenth century, has created an allegory of secular power, depicting the Queen of France in the guise of Minerva.

Jean Goujon (1510–1568)
Venus and Cupid. Mid-16th century. Marble. 51 x 57 cm
(Hall 274)
Goujon, an outstanding sculptor of the Renaissance era skilfully subordinated the figures to the rhythm of the running wave, attaining a sense of lightness, elegance, brightness and joy.

Nicolas Poussin (1594–1665). *Landscape with Polyphemus.* 1649
Oil on canvas. 150 x 199 cm (Hall 279)
Poussin, a master of Classicism, strove in his paintings to
express lofty ideals, following the art of the Ancient World
and the Renaissance. A Poussin landscape is an image of
eternally beautiful nature. The sad melody being played on
the pipes by the cyclops Polyphemus, who is grieving over
unrequited love, invests it with a bright elegiac mood.

Louis Le Nain (1593–1648)
The Milkmaid's Family
1640s. Oil on canvas
51 x 59 cm (Hall 276)
The peasant subject in this,
one of the finest paintings
by Louis Le Nain — the
"painter of reality", is treated in an almost epic man-
ner. His peasants are presented as the embodiment
of wise humility and dignity
against the background of
a landscape that poetically
recreates the gentle natural
beauties of northern France.

Nicolas Poussin (1594–1665). *Tancred and Erminia*. 1630–31
Oil on canvas. 98.5 x 146.5 cm. (Hall 279)
Tancred and Erminia is one of most poetic and sublime works by
Poussin, an emotional affirmation of the beauty of self-sacrifice. Erminia,
the heroine of Torquato Tasso's great poem *Jerusalem Delivered*, is
cutting off her hair, sacrificing its magical power in order to heal
the wounds that Tancred has suffered in a fight with the giant Argant,
the embodiment of evil.

Nicolas Poussin (1594–1665)
Nymph, Satyr and Putti. 1630s
Oil on canvas. 72 x 56 cm
(Hall 279)
This small canvas, actually a study, is
one of the brightest and most joyful
works by Poussin in the Hermitage.
Depicting bacchanalia, the ancient
festival in honour of Bacchus, the god
of wine, Poussin created a harmonious
world with man and nature at one, a
world of freedom and the enjoyment
of earthly beauty. This painting is connected with the series of *Bacchanalia*
that Poussin produced in this period
for Cardinal Richelieu.

**Claude Gellée,
called Lorrain** (1600–1682)
Morning in the Harbour
1640s. Oil on canvas
74 x 97 cm. (Hall 280)
Lorrain lived and worked in
Rome, inspired by the views
of Italy and the ideals of
the great Poussin. A harbour
was one of Lorrain's favourite motifs: he was able to
convey the effects of lighting
through colour, subtly warm-
ing an ideal world of nature.

François Girardon
(1628–1715). *Equestrian
Monument to Louis XIV*
Model. Bronze
Height: 108 cm (Hall 281)
This is the sculptor's own
model of the monument
that stood on the Place
Vendôme in Paris until it
was destroyed during the
French Revolution.

Antoine Watteau
(1684–1721). *An Embarrassing Proposal*. Circa 1716
Oil on canvas. 65 x 84.5 cm
(Hall 284)
This work belongs to the *fête galante* genre that Watteau invented. The title of the work, given to it by one of Watteau's friends, does not reflect its contents: it is not the actions of the personages, but an elusive play of moods that is here conveyed with exquisite line and a wealth of colour.

Antoine Watteau (1684–1721)
The Capricious Woman. Circa 1718
Oil on canvas. 42 x 34 cm (Hall 284)
In this *fête galante*, painted with subtle irony and a profound understanding of the nature of feelings, compositional simplicity is combined with richness and refinement of the palette. The intensity of colour in the figures of the beau and the capricious charmer sets off the tender, translucent quality of the shades in the landscape. Subtle moods and feelings have been converted into a lively, thrilling play of colours.

Nicolas Lancret (1690–1743)
The Dancer Camargo. 1730s. Oil on canvas
44 x 55 cm. (Hall 284)
Marie Camargo (1710–1770), a dancer at the Opéra in Paris, was famous for both her gifts as a ballerina and her literary tastes. The young Voltaire dedicated verses to her. Camargo is depicted dancing, in the manner of the theatrical compositions of Watteau, whose pupil Lancret was.

Watteau opened the eighteenth century in French art. Against a background of the pompous academic painting of the "Grand Siècle", he produced small works, drawing their subjects and motifs from life: he recorded these in drawings made from life and repeated them in his painted compositions. Watteau expressed a different conception, new for the time, of the beauty of human feelings and intimate moods. He introduced new themes and images that were taken up by other French painters.

François Boucher
(1703–1770)
*View in the Environs
of Beauvais.* Early 1740s
Oil on canvas. 49 x 58 cm
(Hall 285)
Boucher, the director of
the Royal Academy, first
painter to the King and a
brilliant master of the decorative Rococo style,
worked in the 1740s at the
tapestry factory at Beau-
vais close to Paris, creating
cartoons that provided the
designs for future tapes-
tries. It was there too that
he painted this exquisite
landscape with a genre
scene in the spirit of Watteau in the foreground.

François Boucher (1703–1770)
Pastoral Scene. 1740s.Oil on canvas. 61 x 75 cm. (Hall 285)
Boucher introduced a new genre into painting — the
pastoral, a variation on the theme of Watteau's *fêtes
galantes* treated as a decorative work in the Rococo
style. It is no coincidence that for a time this painting
served as an embellishment of a mirror in one of the
rooms of the Old Hermitage.

Etienne-Maurice Falconet (1716–1791)
Statue of Winter. 1771. Marble
Height: 135 cm. (Hall 286)
Falconet completed this statue in Russia, in St Petersburg to which he had been invited by Catherine II to work on the monument to Peter the Great that became known as "The Bronze Horseman". While he drew inspiration from the classical beauty of ancient statues, Falconet at the same time introduced into the snow-white marble the refinement and subtle sensuality of Rococo art: the monumental forms, faultless proportions and austere features are softened by the graceful femininity of the pose and the touching gesture of the hand that carefully covers the flowers with the hem of the clothing.

Etienne-Maurice Falconet (1716–1791)
Threatening Cupid. 1766–67
Marble. Height: 85 cm. (Hall 285)
Falconet produced this statue in St Petersburg to a commission from Count Stroganov. In it he repeated the famous *Cupid* he had made in 1757 for the Marquise de Pompadour, the mistress of Louis XV. That *Cupid* was intended to adorn a small rotunda pavilion at Versailles — the "Temple of Love". While creating an exquisite decorative work, the sculptor has not, however, sacrificed truth. He had a fine feeling for the human form and managed to depict convincingly in marble the living charm of a child's body, naturalness in movement, pose and gesture, the fetching charm of the sly expression on the face of the young god of love.

Marie-Anne Collot (1748–1821)
Bust of Falconet. 1773. Marble.
Height: 47 cm. (Hall 286)
Collot, Falconet's pupil and assistant, from whose model the head of Peter the Great for the "Bronze Horseman" was cast, created this lively, striking image of her celebrated mentor.

Jean-Marc Nattier (1685–1766)
Lady in Grey. 1750s(?). Oil on canvas
80 x 64 cm. (Hall 286)
One of the creators of the Rococo-style portrait, Nattier sought first and foremost decorative elegance in the depiction,. making virtuoso use of a palette of pearly-grey hues enlivened by tender pink and scarlet accents.

Jean-Baptiste Perroneau
(1715–1783). *Portrait of a Boy with a Book* Mid-1740s. Oil on canvas 63 x 52 cm. (Hall 286) Perroneau depicted the third estate, the French bourgeoisie. He belonged to the trend in French art known as "Enlightening Realism" that sought to express the ideals of the Enlightenment. The boy in the portrait may have been the artist's brother. The book — an attribute of knowledge and work — introduces into the vivid, immediate image of an adolescent a didactic, moralizing element typical of Enlightenment art.

Jean-Jacques Caffieri
(1725–1797). *Portrait of Countess du Barry*
Marble. Height: 56 cm
(Hall 285)
This skilfully worked piece of marble is a portrait of Madame du Barry, the last mistress of Louis XV. The somewhat provocative pose of the model served as an allusion to the extremely humble origins of the "countess".

The Hall of Falconet and French 18th-Century Art (Hall 285)
French eighteenth-century art is displayed in five state drawing rooms created by the architect Alexander Briullov in 1838–39. They belong to a suite of palace halls devoted to Russia's military victories that also includes the Alexander Hall (Hall 282) and the Gallery of 1812 (Hall 197).

Jean-Baptiste Siméon Chardin
(1699–1779). *Grace*. 1744
Oil on canvas. 49.5 x 38.4 cm. (Hall 287)
Chardin's art gave expression to the ideals of the Enlightenment. With great tact and poetic feeling he raises the question of upbringing. The eloquent image of a mother, gently but firmly instilling in her daughters the rules of piety and morality, the charm of the images of the children, the rich beauty of the colours from which the artist has woven this world filled with quiet, cosiness and human goodness — all this makes the work a true masterpiece.

41

Jean-Baptiste Siméon Chardin (1699–1779)
A Washerwoman. 1730s. Oil on canvas
37.5 x 42.7 cm. (Hall 287)

As a counter to the decorative painting of the Rococo style,
Chardin produced genre paintings that depicted the life of
the third estate. The artist's aim was not, however, simply to
record the daily round, but to reflect on the true values of
life that he found in the prose of everyday existence, in
scenes of domestic labour. He turned the washing of laundry
into a colourful spectacle, making the damp air, the tub of
soapy water and the figures of the women performing an
accustomed task into a precious piece of painting affirming
the beauty of the simple things on which the world depends.
The idea of the nobility of human labour also lies behind
Chardin's late still lifes that are devoted to his reflections on
art. These became very well known and in 1766 Chardin was
commissioned to paint a "still life with attributes of the
arts" by the St Petersburg Academy of Arts.

Jean-Baptiste Siméon Chardin (1699–1779) *Still Life with Attributes of the Arts.* 1766
Oil on canvas
112 x 140.5 cm (Hall 287)
Presented in neat order on the canvas are the tools of the Artist's trade — brushes, paints, sketch-books, architectural drawings, books, and also awards. But it is not these last, but the sculptural model of Mercury by Pigalle (presented by him to Chardin) that is the crowning element of the composition, as if insisting that the artist's highest reward is his own work, the fruit of his talent and labour.

Jean-Antoine Houdon (1741–1828). *Voltaire Seated in an Armchair.* 1781
Marble. Height: 138 cm (Hall 287)
This statue is the sculptor's own repetition of the famous creation on which Houdon began work shortly before Voltaire's death. Today the original stands in the foyer of the Comédie Française theatre in Paris. Houdon produced an image full of life and significance of the intelligent, perspicacious, ironic thinker — the leading intellectual figure of his time. The Hermitage statue was commissioned from Houdon by Catherine II. She wanted it to adorn the pavilion at Tsarskoye Selo in which she planned to house Voltaire's library that she had purchased after the philosopher's death. That plan was not realised, however. The statue remained in the Hermitage, while Voltaire's books were subsequently transferred to the Public Library in St Petersburg.

43

Jean-Honoré Fragonard (1732–1806). *The Forfeited Kiss*. Oil on canvas 47 x 60 cm. (Hall 288) Fragonard is reckoned a master of the Rococo. It was, however, not the decorative effects of the style and not the piquancy of the situation, but the joyful, sensual feeling of life captured in the free use of the brush, in the bold unfinished drawing, in the daring contrasts of light and shade that made him one of the most brilliant painters French in the eighteenth century.

Jean-Honoré Fragonard (1732–1806). *A Stolen Kiss* Oil on canvas. 45 x 55 cm (Hall 288) The exquisitely arranged little scene betrays an artist who learnt the techniques of the Rococo from the creator of the style, Boucher, while the persuasiveness with which the figures, objects and fabrics have been painted is evidence of lessons taken from the leader of Enlightening Realism, Chardin. Still, all this is only an obedient tool in the hands of a great talent.

Jean-Baptiste Greuze (1725–1805) *The Paralytic*. 1763. Oil on canvas 115.5 x 146 cm. (Hall 288) This painting made Greuze famous. It was fervently praised in an article by the philosopher Denis Diderot who called the artist's painting "moral". On the eve of the revolution Greuze's paintings came across as a declaration of the virtues of the common man in contrast to the depravity of the French aristocracy. Catherine II bought this painting on Diderot's advice.

Tapestry: *May. The Chateau of Saint-Germain. The King Strolling with Ladies* **From the series *The Months, or the Royal Châteaux.*** Late 17th – early 18th century Royal Gobelins Factory, Paris. Wool and silk. 318 x 291 cm. (Hall 292)
The cartoons for this series were produced in the years 1666–69 from sketches by the head of the Royal Academy, Charles Le Brun (1619–1690).

André-Charles Boulle (1642–1732)
Cabinet. Second half of the 17th century Paris. Ebony with gilded bronze, marquetry 255 x 170 x 64 cm. (Hall 292)
The chief cabinetmaker to King Louis XIV, Boulle personally hammered and gilded the bronze decorations for his pieces and assembled the elaborate patterns on the doors from sheets of precious wood and brass. Later the methods of decoration that he devised came to be known by his name.

Secretaire. Circa 1760
Made by Dubut, Paris
Rosewood inlaid with
ivory and mother-of-pearl
144 x11 x 48 cm
(Hall 294)
This secretaire with wave-
shaped patterned lids in
exquisite frames of gilded
bronze is one of the masterpieces of Rococo-style
furniture.

Cameo Service
1778–79. Sèvres, France
Soft porcelain. (Hall 297)
In France the first porcelain
began to be produced in
the middle of the eight-
eenth century. In 1756 the
royal factory was founded
at Sèvres. It produced items
made of soft porcelain (fired
at a lower temperature than
real, or hard porcelain) that
were distinguished by the
brightness of their colours
and the plastic quality of
their lines. Sèvres porcelain
became highly fashionable
in Europe. Catherine II
ordered the Cameo Service
which contains more than
700 items.

The Display of French 17th–18th-Century Applied Art. Detail (Hall 297)
The display allows visitors to trace changes in styles over two centuries. Objects in one of the halls — a table from the Admiralty that was made by Paul I's craftsman Meyer, table ornaments and torchères by the celebrated bronze-smith Pierre-Philippe Thomire (1751–1843), Gobelins tapestries from the *Story of Esther* series, furniture by Adam Weisweiler (1744–1820) with Sèvres porcelain in-sets — give a clear picture of the "Louis XVI" style.

The Display of French 17th–18th-Century Applied Art (Hall 297)
The fashion for French luxury items in the eighteenth century that led to the purchase and commissioning from that country of furniture, tapestries, silver and porcelain for the palace laid the foundations of this collection. It became exceptionally rich and full after the revolution when items from the palaces and museums of St Petersburg were added to it. A particularly valuable acquisition was the collection of Baron Stieglitz, the founder of the College of Technical Drawing, transferred to the Hermitage in 1923.

47

The Apartments
of Empress Maria Alexandrovna

The White Hall begins the suite of living apartments along the south-west facade of the palace that Briullov created for the wedding of Tsesarevich Alexander Nikolayevich, the future Alexander II, and Princess Marie of Hesse-Darmstadt, who took the name Maria Alexandrovna on conversion to Orthodoxy. After becoming Empress in 1855, she continued to live in these rooms until her death in 1880. The apartments have retained the original artistic appearance from the mid-nineteenth century and provide a typical example of how the living quarters were arranged in a royal residence.

FIRST FLOOR

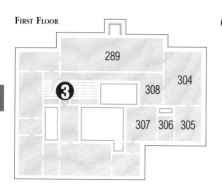

❸ OCTOBER STAIRCASE (ACCESS TO THE GROUNDFLOOR), WOODEN STAIRCASE (ACCESS TO THE SECOND FLOOR)

This state room belonging to the living apartments of Empress Maria Alexandrovna is one of Alexander Briullov's finest works as an architect. Flooded with light from windows placed in two tiers, the snow-white walls and vaults are generously adorned by moulded ornament, Corinthian columns and sculpture.

The works from the last decades of the eighteenth century complete the display of early French art. They include notably the paintings of French artist who worked in Russia — Jean-Louis Voille (1744–1804) and Elisabeth Vigée-Lebrun (1755–1842). The latter, known for her portraits of Queen Marie Antoinette, found refuge and employment at the Russian court following the French Revolution.

The White Hall also contains furniture made by the celebrated German-born craftsman David Roentgen (1743–1800). His massive desks of elaborate design usually incorporate bookrests, a host of drawers and secret compartments. They are equipped with clever mechanisms, including musical ones.

The White Hall. 1838–41
Architect: Alexander Briullov
(Hall 289)

William Brown (1748–1825). England
The Head of Hygeia. Cornelian set in gold
3 x 2.7 cm. (Hall 304)
Hygeia was the Greek goddess of health,
daughter of Asclepius, the god of healing.

Portrait of Henry IV. 1596. France
Mother of pearl. 2.2 x 1.7 cm. (Hall 304)
Henry IV reigned in France from 1594 to 1610

Giovanni Pichler. 1734–1791. Italy
A Centaur and a Bacchante
Second half of the 18th century
Sardonyx. 1.7 x 2.4 cm. (Hall 304)

Cameo: *Mars and Venus*
1530s. France. Carved seashell
7.8 x 6.5 cm (without the mount)

> **The Gold Drawing-Room.** 1860s
Architect: Alexander Briullov. (Hall 304)

The art of engraving on precious and semiprecious stones has its origins in deep antiquity. Behind it lies a belief in the miraculous power of the stone, a desire to turn it into an amulet, by carving upon it magic signs and images, later portraits and elaborate multi-figure compositions. Glyptics reached its height in the Ancient Mediterranean world. Its techniques, subjects and traditions were then taken up by Western European craftsmen. In Europe this branch of art was at its peak particularly during the Renaissance era. The Gold Drawing-Room of the Winter Palace houses examples of Western European glyptics. They come from an rich collection of over 10,000 carved gems, both intaglios, where the design is concave (like a seal), and cameos, where the design is convex, created by craftsmen from a number of countries.

The Crimson Drawing-Room (or Study). Late 1850s
Architect: Andrei Stakenschneider. (Hall 305)
Stakenschneider created this drawing-room in the place
of Briullov's state study for the Empress. The walls of the
room are lined with dark red silk fabric that was recreated in the 1950s, following the wartime siege, from
authentic nineteenth-century samples. The medallions
containing notes and musical instruments in the pattern
of the fabric are reminders that the room was used as
a music-room. The Empress, who was a connoisseur of
art, also used it to house her favourite paintings (transferred to the Hermitage after her death), including Raphael's *Conestabile Madonna*, given to her by her husband,
Alexander II. The Crimson Drawing-Room is a cosier,
more intimate place than the preceding grand Gold
Drawing-Room (Hall 304) which was redecorated
in the 1860s by the architect Vladimir Schreiber.

The Green Dining-Room. 1850
Architect: Andrei Stakenschneider. (Hall 308)
With his great knowledge of the architecture of the past and
subtle ability to stylize, Stakenschneider used the techniques
of the French Rococo here to create an elegant, welcoming
interior adorned with whimsical moulded ornament, painted
panels and mirrors. The room has no windows. In daytime
light entered through a skylight, giving a particular atmosphere of intimacy to the family dining-room. Maria Alexandrovna was the mother of eight children and diligently concerned herself with their upbringing.

The Boudoir. 1853
Architect: Harald Bosse. (Hall 306)
Bosse reworked Briullov's Boudoir in the
style of the Rococo: gilded rocaille frames
enclose fabric panels and mirrors, visually
expanding the relatively small interior.

The Blue Bedroom. 1838–41
Architect: Alexander Briullov. (Hall 308)
Maria Alexandrovna was very fond of the
Classically austere, somewhat gloomy decoration that Briullov created for her bedroom with its dark blue walls and cur-
tains. Today the bedroom houses a display
of the creations of jewellers.

> The October Staircase. 1830s
Architect: Auguste Montferrand
Maria Alexandrovna's apartments were
entered by way of Her Imperial Majesty's
Entrance and Staircase. Today both bear
the name October in commemoration of
the events of that month in 1917 when
the palace, then the seat of the Provisional Government, was stormed.

Germany, 15th–18th Centuries
Department of Western European Art

In Catherine II's time, the halls that now house the collection of fifteenth- to eighteenth-century German art were service rooms used by the state secretaries. Here too the Empress's trusted friend and lady-in-waiting Maria Perekusikhina had her rooms.

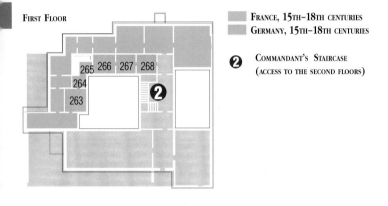

FIRST FLOOR

FRANCE, 15TH–18TH CENTURIES
GERMANY, 15TH–18TH CENTURIES

❷ COMMANDANT'S STAIRCASE
(ACCESS TO THE SECOND FLOORS)

Although of considerable size, containing as it does some 700 paintings, 100 sculptures and over 30,000 prints as well as many works of applied art, the collection of German art is nevertheless not as complete or as whole as others in the Department of Western European art. The first works from the German Renaissance, a brief but bright highpoint in German culture, came to St Petersburg mainly in the eighteenth century. Some of them belonged to the large collections bought up by Catherine the Great, but at that time they were not the object of specific collecting. There was just as little interest back then in seventeenth-century German art. In Catherine's reign there was a vogue for the works of Anton Raphael Mengs, one of the founders of the Neo-Classical movement popular in late-eighteenth-century Europe. As a result the Hermitage has a first-rate collection of works by the artist himself and his contemporaries.

Unknown artist of the North German School of the early 15th century
Christ at the Last Judgement with Interceding Mary and John the Baptist
Tempera on panel. 46.5 x 70 cm. (Hall 263)
This is the earliest example of German painting in the Hermitage. The image of Christ as a dispassionate judge to whom Mary and John the Baptist pray for the for-

giveness of human sins was usually commissioned for courtrooms. The attributes are of tremendous significance: the lily is associated with the Immaculate Conception, the sword with the power of justice, Christ's wounds and the instruments of the Passion held by the angels with His mission of Redemption. Works of this kind were intended to remind judges to be just in their verdicts.

Ambrosius Holbein (ca. 1495 – ca. 1520)
Portrait of a Young Man. 1518
Oil and tempera on panel. 44 x 32.5 cm (Hall 263)
Ambrosius Holbein, a son and pupil of Hans Holbein the Elder, worked for a time with his brother, the great portraitist Hans Holbein the Younger. His paintings are rarities as Ambrosius died young, without even reaching the age of thirty. This portrait of a young man was probably painted in the Swiss city of Basle, to which the brothers moved in 1515. Every detail of the work points to the artist's deep fascination with Italian art. The ancient column speaks of his interest in antiquity. The luxurious Italian palazzo behind the subject's back is a nod of appreciation to the art of the Renaissance. The cartouche attached to the column on the left refers to the portrait and its subject and reads: "at the age of 20, 1518".

**> Lucas Cranach
the Elder** (1472–1553)
Venus and Cupid. 1509
Oil on canvas (transferred
from panel in 1850)
213 x 102 cm. (Hall 264)
This painting is a masterpiece from the early period
in the career of the great
German artist of the Ren-
aissance era. It is believed
that the Hermitage paint-
ing was the first attempt
made in Northern Europe
to depict the goddess of
love and beauty in the
nude. There is deliberate
tension in the goddess's
pose and in the detached
look on her face. In Germany at the time of the Refor-
mation, the pagan goddess
of love was a symbol of
the sin of sensuality. Hence
the Latin inscription in the
upper part of the work that
reads: "Drive off Cupid's
venery with all your might,
lest Venus gain possession
of your blinded soul."

**>> Lucas Cranach
the Elder** (1472–1553)
*The Virgin and Child under
the Apple-Tree.* 1528
Oil on canvas (transferred
from panel). 87 x 59 cm
(Hall 264)
Cranach's paintings convey
the highly distinctive quality of German sixteenth-
century art, when the stern
religious spirit of the Ref-
ormation combined har-
moniously with the ideas
of Humanism and national
folklore. Cranach's golden-

haired Virgin looks like a princess from a German fairy-tale and is depicted in a true
landscape of paradise. The fruit-laden branches of the apple-tree encircle her head like
a magnificent crown. The subject of the painting is an interpretation of the Christian
dogma of the Fall and salvation of the human race. The apple and the bread being held
by the Christ-Child are a symbol of the redemption.

Lucas Cranach the Elder (1472–1553)
Portrait of a Lady. 1526. Oil on panel. 88.5 x 58.6 cm
(Hall 264)
Most probably the woman whose image contains features
beloved by the artist was not a real model. Some scholars
have, however, tried to associate this image with Sybille
of Cleves, the bride of Johann-Friedrich of Saxony. Cranach, as court artist to the King of Saxony, would be ex-
pected to extol the beauty of the monarch's chosen consort. The artist displays an amazing mastery in conveying
the complicated patterns of the costume and jewellery.

Bartolomäus Bruyn the Elder (1493–1555)
Portrait of a Man and His Three Sons
Late 1530s – early 1540s. Oil on canvas
(transferred from panel). 75.5 x 46 cm
(Hall 264)

Bartolomäus Bruyn the Elder (1493–1555)
Portrait of a Woman and Her Daughter
Late 1530s – early 1540s
Oil on canvas (transferred from panel)
75:5 x 46 cm. (Hall 264)
Bruyn the Elder was a noted portrait-
painter based in Cologne who was in
great demand with clients, especially rich
merchants. The two Hermitage portraits
are typical paired images of a family executed following the tradition of the Low
Countries.

Georg Flegel (1566–1638). *Still Life with
Flowers and Food.* Oil on panel. 52.5 x 41 cm
(Hall 267)
Flegel is a well-known German master of
the still life. His painting is marked by a
wholly German thoroughness and scrupu-
lousness in the reproduction of detail.

61

Adam Elsheimer
(1578–1610)
Saint Christopher
Oil on copper. 22.5 x 17.5 cm
(Hall 266)
Elsheimer spent almost all
his creative career in Italy
where he was considerably
better known and recog-
nized than in his home-
land. Rubens, Rembrandt
and Poussin were admirers
of his works.
The subject of the Hermitage's only painting by this
artist is taken from the
legend of a pagan strong-
man who on the advice of
a hermit undertook to carry people across a stream.
Once a child he was taking
across became so heavy
that he felt like he was
carrying the whole weight
of the world and realised
that he had Christ Himself
on his shoulders. Christopher began to preach
Christianity and died
a martyr's death.

Jurgen Ovens (1623–1679)
Self-Portrait of the Artist at the Easel
Oil on canvas. 125 x 95 cm
(Hall 267)
Ovens studied in Holland, apparently in
the studio of Rembrandt. Together with
Rembrandt, Govert Flinck and Jan Lievens
he produced paintings for the Amsterdam
town-hall. He worked in his homeland
and Sweden as well as Holland. The artist
was known for his portraits, and also for
works on religious and historical subjects.

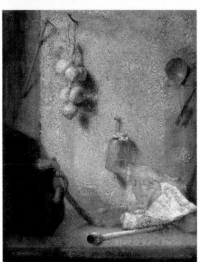

Christopher Paudiss (ca. 1618–1666)
Still Life. 1660. Oil on canvas (transferred from panel)
62 x 46.5 cm (Hall 267)
Paudiss lived in Holland in the 1640s and may have been
a pupil of Rembrandt for a time because his still life is painted with the poetic realism that characterized the finest
Dutch works in the seventeenth century. The everyday, un-
prepossessing objects making up a typical "kitchen still life"
are bathed in a golden light. Their outlines are devoid of
preciseness, the volumes seem to be dissolving in the space,
making a single whole with the surrounding atmosphere.

Daniel Schultz
(1615–1683)
*Portrait of a Polish Aristocrat
with His Son and Servants*
1654(?) or 1664(?)
Oil on canvas. 166 x 231 cm
(Hall 267)
Daniel Schultz spent al-
most his entire life outside
Germany. In the 1640s he
worked in the Netherlands
and in the 1660s became
court painter to King John
II Casimir of Poland in
Warsaw. It was formerly
believed that this picture
depicted the Polish aristocrat Michal Radziwill and
his sons. There were, however, also other titles — *A
Kalmyk and His Family* and
A Tatar Family — obviously
based on the Mongoloid
features of the subjects.
The column bears a half-
effaced inscription including, indistinctly, the date
of painting.

The Hall of Eighteenth-Century German Art. (Hall 268)
Works of art from the eighteenth century account for the greater part of the Hermitage's German collection. Catherine II actively purchased the works of then-fashionable German painters. For example, on her instructions in 1779, immediately after the death of Adam Raphael Mengs, a large group of paintings by the celebrated artist were bought from his studio in Rome. A year later the Hermitage's most famous work by Mengs, *Perseus and Andromeda*, was brought to St Petersburg from Paris. It has a very interesting history. They say that Mengs painted the work to a commission from some Englishman in 1777 and put it on display in his Rome studio to general delight. The following year the painting was sent to England by sea, but the ship was seized by French pirates. Mengs's work turned up in the Spanish port of Cadiz, where it was sold to the French naval minister; Catherine then acquired it from him through the agency of the noted encyclopaedist Melchior Grimm.

Anton Raphael Mengs
(1728–1779)
Perseus and Andromeda
1777. Oil on canvas
227 x 153.5 cm. (Hall 268)
In *Perseus and Andromeda*
an artist who was in love
with ancient sculpture
literally copied onto canvas the finest marble
models of the great era.
His splendid Perseus is
reminiscent of the statue
of Apollo Belvedere, while
the pose and movement of
Andromeda were borrowed
from an ancient relief.

Angelica Kauffmann (1741–1807)
Self-Portrait. Between 1780 and 1785
Oil on canvas. 76.5 x 63 cm. (Hall 268)
Angelica Kauffmann did not receive
systematic professional training, yet
thanks to her talent and her persistent
copying of classical prototypes in Italy
she achieved great successes, became
a famous portrait-painter, a member
of the Academy of St Luke in Rome and
the only female member of the Royal
Academy in London. There are few artists from German-speaking countries
who managed to attain such poeticism,
freshness and lyricism as fills Kauffmann's works. The best aspects of this
artists talent are exhibited not in her
pictures, which are marked by a certain
over-rationality and theatricality, but
first and foremost in her vivid, emotional portraits that enjoyed enormous
popularity with contemporaries.

England, 16th–19th Centuries
Department of Western European Art

The halls that house the display of English art of the sixteenth to nineteenth centuries were restored after the fire of 1837 as a reserve living apartment. It was occupied by Nicholas I's daughter Maria and her husband, the Duke of Leuchtenberg, for a time after their wedding, while the Mariinsky Palace was being completed. In the later nineteenth century the suite was known as the Fourth Reserve Apartment.

First Floor

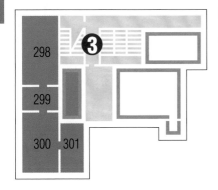

ENGLAND, 16TH–19TH CENTURIES

3 OCTOBER STAIRCASE
(ACCESS TO THE GROUNDFLOOR),
WOODEN STAIRCASE
(ACCESS TO THE SECOND FLOOR)

In the eighteenth century Russia was perhaps the only country in Europe to take a serious interest in English art. The work of English painters was then little known on the continent. The large collection of Robert Walpole that Catherine II acquired included works by his countrymen and these formed the basis for the future section of the Hermitage collection. By the end of the century that section had already been expanded with a number of famous works commissioned by the Empress from celebrated contemporary English artists, most notably Joshua Reynolds and Joseph Wright of Derby. In the nineteenth century interest in English art grew considerably and the works of artists representing that nation's culture appeared in private St Petersburg collections. In 1912 the Hermitage picture gallery received a generous bequest in the form of the collection of English painting assembled by the noted St Petersburg collector Alexei Khitrovo. It is to this that the Hermitage owes some remarkable works by outstanding portraitists of the eighteenth and early nineteenth centuries, above all, masterpieces by Thomas Gainsborough.

England, 16th–19th Centuries

The Hall of English Art of the 16th to 17th centuries
(Hall 298)
The majority of paintings displayed in the halls are portraits. From the sixteenth century onwards portraiture was considered the leading genre in English art. Only in the late seventeenth and early eighteenth century did English painting approach the heyday that is associated with three outstanding figures — William Hogarth, Joshua Reynolds and Thomas Gainsborough. Sadly, the Hermitage does not possess any works by Hogarth.

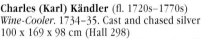

Charles (Karl) Kändler (fl. 1720s–1770s)
Wine-Cooler. 1734–35. Cast and chased silver
100 x 169 x 98 cm (Hall 298)
This wine-cooler was produced in London. The decoration draws on ancient motifs deriving from myths about Dionysus, the Ancient Greek god of wine and wine-making. The handles of the huge silver vessel take the form of satyrs and bacchantes, the companions of the god. The bowl rests on the backs of four panthers who are attached together with chains. The side walls are adorned with relief images featuring dancing cupids, while the rim of the vessel is entwined with a superbly chased silver grapevine. This virtuoso example of the silversmith's art weighs over 200 kilogrammes (some 450 pounds).

Paul de Lamérie
(1688–1751)
Wine-Fountain. 1720–21
Cast and chased silver
Height: 70 cm
This exquisite piece is one of the earliest works by the celebrated London-based Huguenot jeweller Paul de Lamerie. Wine poured into such a vessel would remain cool for a long time.

Julien de Fontenay(?)
(worked in France and England in the last quarter of the 16th century)
Portrait of Elizabeth Tudor
Cameo. *Ca.* 1575. Sardonyx in a gold mount (18th century). 6.2 x 4.7 cm
This cameo came into the Hermitage collection in 1787 from France, as part of the remarkable collection of carved gemstones assembled by the Duc d'Orléans. Of the six Hermitage cameos bearing depictions of the great English Queen, this is the best in terms of quality and size.

Marcus Geeraerts the Younger(?)
(1561/62 – 1635/36)
Portrait of an Unknown Man. 1595
Oil on panel. 114.5 x 89 cm
(Hall 298)
The portrait is painted in the smooth, flat, stylized manner characteristic of the reign of Elizabeth I (1558–1603). The inscription tells us that it was made in 1595 when the subject was 32 years old. Marcus Geeraerts studied under his father who had moved to England from Flanders. By the early seventeenth century he had become one of England's leading artists and was appointed painter to the King. It is, however, difficult to attribute this work to Geeraerts with complete certainty, as the portrait is unsigned and the artist's manner of painting was not particularly distinctive.

Godfrey Kneller
(1646/49(?) – 1723)
Portrait of Grinling Gibbons
No later than 1690
Oil on canvas. 125 x 90 cm
(Hall 298)
Grinling Gibbons (1648–1720) was a sculptor who earned a brilliant reputation with his carvings in lime wood, chiefly garlands and other decorative elements containing fruit, vases and flowers.

William Dobson
(1611–1646)
Portrait of Abraham van der Doort. Late 1630s
Oil on canvas. 45 x 38 cm
(Hall 298)
Dobson was one of the most gifted portrait-painters working in England in the seventeenth century. Abraham van der Doort was a medallist who served Charles I as curator of

Henry Raeburn (1756–1823)
Portrait of Eleanor Bethune. 1790s
Oil on canvas. 76 x 64 cm (Hall 298)
Sir Henry Raeburn was a celebrated Scottish artist. His restrained, laconic portraits still emanage to expressively convey character and mood.

paintings and curiosities. Van der Doort's life ended tragically in 1640: he committed suicide after discovering the loss of a miniature that Charles had entrusted to him as especially valuable.

George Romney
(1734–1802)
Portrait of Harriet Greer
1781. Oil on canvas
76 x 64 cm. (Hall 298)
The noted English portrait-painted George Romney was a a younger contemporary of Reynolds and Gainsborough. Unable to reach the heights of fame attained by the leading artists of the century, he was nevertheless very popular with clients in London, especially women. The artist could superbly convey in his portraits the elegance, social charm and refinement of the female members of Britain's social elite.

John Hoppner
(1758–1810)
Portrait of Richard Sheridan(?)
Late 1780s – early 1790s
Oil on canvas. 77 x 64 cm
(Hall 298)
Like Romney, Hoppner possessed considerable professional skill and in his work followed in the footsteps of Reynolds and Gainsborough. Richard Brinsley Sheridan was a famous dramatist, the author of the celebrated *School for Scandal*, an orator and public figure. Specialists who have compared Hoppner's work with the more precise likeness of Sheridan painted by Reynolds have expressed doubts as to whether Sheridan did actually pose for the artist, since no reliable record of him doing so survives.

Thomas Gainsborough (1727–1788)
Portrait of a Lady in Blue. Late 1770s
Oil on canvas. 76 x 64 cm. (Hall 298)
When it entered the Hermitage collection in 1916, this masterpiece by Thomas Gainsborough was designated as a portrait of the Duchesse de Beaufort, wife of the French ambassador to the English court. There is, however, no record of the artist ever having painted any member of the ambassador's family. To this day the beautiful unknown woman, sublime like some Romantic dream, remains the mysterious, puzzling Lady in Blue. Gainsborough was one of the most remarkable painters of the eighteenth century. His work is striking for its wealth of colour nuances and virtuoso technique, while his models are marked by particular refinement, poeticality and spirituality of feelings — qualities present in full measure in the artist himself.

Joseph Wright of Derby (1743–1797). *Fireworks. The Castel Sant'Angelo in Rome (Girandole).* 1775–79 Oil on canvas. 162.5 x 213 cm (Hall 299)

Joseph Wright of Derby is rightly considered one of the most original of English eighteenth-century artists. This painting, together with its companion piece *The Eruption of Vesuvius* (now in the Pushkin Fine Arts Museum, Moscow) was acquired in the artist's studio for Catherine II. In Rome, Wright witnessed the celebratory fireworks (girandoles) that were set off on the roof of Castel Sant'Angelo. Later the artist went on to Naples, where he saw an eruption of Mount Vesuvius. Under the impression of these two tremendous fiery spectacles he created his paired set of paintings.

Joseph Wright of Derby (1734–1797). *An Iron Forge Viewed from Without.* 1773. Oil on canvas. 105 x 140 cm (Hall 299)

Wright, who lived in Derby, one of England's major industrial centres, was interested in scenes from everyday life in which he strove to convey the special significance and importance of the physical life of human beings and their surroundings. One such painting — *An Iron Forge Viewed from Without* — is a real-life scene that the artist turned into a poetic, slightly mysterious, romantic elegy in which the main protagonists are not the people, but the fascinating play of light and shade in nature.

Josiah Wedgwood (1730–1795)
Items from the Green Frog Service. 1773–74
Earthenware, overglaze painting. (Hall 300)
This service was commissioned by Catherine II for the wayside palace (later called the Chesme Palace) that stood on the southern outskirts of St Petersburg. The local Finnish population called the area Kekerekesinen, meaning "the frog marsh". Hence the emblem on the service — a green frog in a heraldic shield. The service was designed for fifty people and included dinner (650 pieces decorated with garlands of oak leaves) and desert (264 items farmed with ivy garlands) sets. The painted scene worked in purple on a creamy white background on each item is a specific, topographically precise view of some place in England.

George Morland
(1763–1804)
Approaching Thunderstorm.
1791. Oil on canvas
85 x 117 cm (Hall 299)
In a short lifetime George Morland produced some 4,000 paintings, mainly landscapes and genre scenes.
Approaching Thunderstorm, one of the best works in his legacy anticipates the discoveries of the Romantics.

Joshua Reynolds
(1723–1792)
The Infant Hercules Strangling the Serpents. 1786–88
Oil on canvas. 303 x 297 cm
In December 1785 Joshua Reynolds, the most influential English artist of the eighteenth century, received a flattering request from the Russian court to paint two works on a historical subject. One was intended for Empress Catherine, the other for her favourite Prince Potemkin. In choosing a subject from Classical mythology Reynolds invested it with a deeper meaning — the scene is an allegory glorifying the power and might of the young Russian state. According to the myth, Hera, the jealous wife of the chief Greek deity Zeus, decided to dispose of the son born to Zeus by the mortal Alcmene and sent two huge serpents to kill him in the cradle. Awoken by their cold touch Hercules (or Heracles) performed his first exploit and strangled them.

The Hall of 18th-Century English Art (Hall 300)
Besides the works of Reynolds, the hall also contains formal portraits by English artists as well as silver and porcelain.

England, 16th–19th Centuries

Benjamin West
(1738–1820)
Venus Consoling Cupid Who Has Been Stung by a Bee. Late 1790s. Oil on canvas 77 x 64 cm. (Hall 300)
The artist found this subject in an ode by the ancient Greek poet Anacreon entitled *The Wounded Cupid*, and the programmatic work that he produced original had a longer title that completely explained the scene: *Cupid stung on the finger by a bee. Venus* As a true Neo-Classicist, West was absorbed with "reconstructing" ideal ancient images on canvas and carefully, but coldly delineates the splendid profile of the goddess of beauty, but the image of the weeping Cupid and the bright, pale blue and pink palette give the scene a certain sentimental tone.

Joshua Reynolds
(1723–1792)
Cupid Untying the Girdle of Venus. 1788. Oil on canvas 77 x 64 cm. (Hall 300)
This work, the artist's own replica of this famous 1784 painting now in the Tate Gallery in London, is a remarkable example of Reynolds's free improvising manner and his rich palette of colours. Reynolds's Venus is far from the ideal of Classical beauty. In her guise we are presented with a splendid read-haired English model who may have been Emma Hart, later the beautiful, romantic Lady Hamilton, who posed for the artist twice in her youth.

Richard Parkes Bonington (1802–1828). *Boats by the Normandy Coast. Ca.* 1825 Oil on canvas. 33.5 x 46 cm (Hall 301)

Bonington spent the greater part of his short life in France. His intimate, small-sized landscapes, marked by a free improvising manner of execution and a subtle use of colour attracted the attention of Parisian art-lovers.

Christina Robertson (1775–1856) *Children with a Parrot* 1850s. Oil on canvas. 112 x 104 cm (Hall 301) Sentimentality and the chocolate-box prettiness of the Salon were the hallmarks of portraits by Christina Robinson, making her a welcome guest in the high society of St Petersburg, Vienna and Berlin.

England, 16th–19th Centuries

Thomas Lawrence
(1769–1830)
Portrait of Lady Emily Harriet Fitzroy. Ca. 1815
Oil on panel. 73 x 63 cm
(Hall 301)
Thomas Lawrence was the most prominent English portraitist of the early nineteenth century. Almost all the crowned heads of Europe as well as military and diplomatic celebrities sat for him. A brilliant master of the formal portrait, he could depict any client full of emotion, energy and passion. Emily Harriet Fitzroy was a niece of Wellington and the wife of Lord Fitzroy-Somerset, later Lord Raglan, the commander-in-chief of the British army in the Crimean War of 1853–56.

Thomas Lawrence
(1769–1830). *Portrait of Count Mikhail Vorontsov.* 1821. Oil on canvas 143 x 113 cm (Hall 301)
Count Mikhail Vorontsov, accorded the title of illustrious prince in 1853, was a major military and public figure, the governor general of New Russia (the Ukraine) and from 1856 Field Marshal General. He spent his childhood and youth in England where his father, Count Semion Vorontsov, was Russian ambassador for more than forty years. In 1819 Vorontsov travelled to London with his young wife to visit his father. While there he commissioned a formal portrait from Lawrence. The Count is depicted in a general's uniform with the badges of three Russian orders: St Alexander Nevsky, St Vladimir and St George.

France, 19th–20th Centuries

Department of Western European Art

More than 25 halls on the top floor of the Winter Palace are given over to the display of French art of the nineteenth and twentieth centuries. This is an enormous collection giving a developing picture of the main stages, tendencies and leading figures in French art from the time of the Revolution, that became a dividing line between old and new culture, to the First World War. The revolution that followed in Russia cut off the country's contacts with Western art and the entry of individual post-1917 works into the Hermitage has been episodic in character.

▨ France, 19th–20th Centuries	❷ Commandant's Staircase
▨ Germany, Italy and other european countries, 19th–20th Centuries	(access to the first floor)
	❸ Wooden Staircase
	(access to the first floor)

Second Floor

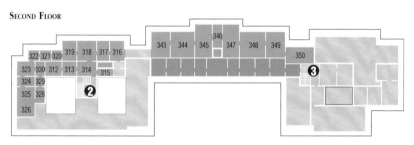

This collection appeared in the Hermitage only after the 1917 revolution. In the nineteenth century the Imperial Hermitage did not acquire contemporary art. It was the object of private collecting. The private collections nationalized after the revolution and given to the Hermitage formed a "modern" art section in the museum. The imperial palaces and mansions of the St Petersburg nobility provided numerous works of academic and salon art. The over 300 paintings in the collection of Count Kushelev-Bezborodko (1837–1862) that were transferred to the Hermitage from the Academy of Arts in 1922 formed the basis for the section covering the first half of the nineteenth century — works by the Romantics and Barbizon school landscapes. The Hermitage owes its world-famous collection of paintings by the Impressionists, Post-Impressionists and the European avant-garde to the Muscovite collectors of the turn of the twentieth century Sergei Shchukin (1854–1936) and Ivan Morozov (1871–1921). The State Museum of New Western Art that was created in Moscow after the revolution on the basis of their collections was disbanded in 1948 as "alien to the people". The stocks were threatened with destruction, but were saved by the intervention of the Hermitage and the Pushkin Museum of Fine Arts in Moscow. They took in the collections for safekeeping, dividing them between themselves. The Hermitage also acquired some other private collections, as well as individual works donated, bequeathed or purchased by the museum.

Jean Antoine Gros (1771–1835)
Napoleon on the Bridge at Arcole. 1797
Oil on canvas. 134 x 104 cm (Hall 314)
Nineteenth-century art was born in
France even before the new century began, together with the terrible events of
the French Revolution and the Napoleonic Wars. The sheer immensity of the era
brought artists back to the great ideals of
Classical Antiquity, but it was not ancient
history, but dramatic contemporary reality that became their source of heroic

images. The hero taken by Gros, a major
exponent of Neo-Classicism, was the
young general Napoleon Bonaparte, urg-
ing his soldiers into battle at Arcole on
the River Adige on 16 November 1796.
This version of the painting (two others
are in the Louvre and at Versailles) belonged at one time to Napoleon's step-
son, Eugène Beauharnais, and was
brought to Russia by one of his descend-
ants, Duke Maximilian of Leuchtenberg,
who married a daughter of Nicholas I.

Jacques-Louis David (1748–1825)
Sappho and Phaon. 1809
Oil on canvas. 225.3 x 262 cm (Hall 332)
Love is a rare theme in the art of David, the
leader of the Neo-Classical trend. Working
to a commission from Prince Yusupov he
created a sublime, if somewhat chilly ra-
tional, image of the Ancient Greek poetess
Sappho, whose love for the youth Phaon,
became a source of her inspiration.

Jean Auguste Dominique Ingres
(1780–1867). *Portrait of Count Guryev*
1821. Oil on canvas. 107 x 86 cm
(Hall 331)
Ingres, a pupil of David, a great master
of line, was a custodian of the traditions
of Classicism and an enemy of Romanticism in painting. Nevertheless he depicted
the Russian aristocrat Nikolai Guryev
(1792–1849) as a wholly "Romantic hero"
– bored, disillusioned with the mark of
hidden passions on the well-bred face.

François Gérard (1770–1837)
Portrait of Josephine. 1801
Oil on canvas. 178 x 174 cm
(Hall 314)
This portrait of Josephine, the "beautiful creole" who became the wife of General Napoleon Bonaparte, was painted three years before she became empress. Josephine is shown on the terrace of her favourite palace, Malmaison. Gérard, an artist of David's school and a fashionable portraitist of the Napoleonic elite, softened the cold elegance of the Empire style with a Romantic mood created by the mysterious landscape, the relaxed pose and the great significance of the details.

Romanticism was not simply a vogue. It was prevailing the sense of the world in a rapidly changing eras that gave rise to outbursts and turmoil in people's emotions, fuelling passions and disappointments. This perception of the world engendered the freedom-seeking art of the French Romantics. The Romantic tendency that emerged in France in the first twenty years of the nineteenth century, is represented in the Hermitage by works that are few in number, but striking.

Eugène Delacroix (1798–1863). *A Lion Hunt in Morocco*. 1854
Oil on canvas. 74 x 92 cm. (Hall 313)
The Hermitage has two masterpieces by the great Romantic Delacroix,
late works inspired by memories of his journey to Morocco that took
place in 1832, twenty years before the canvases were painted. The foremost French Romanticist retained to the end of his days the Romantic
excitement and vividness of perception that find expression in the bold
contrasts of colour and unrestrained, energetic brushwork.

Antoine Louis Barye
(1796–1875). *A Lion*
Bronze. Height: 50 cm
(Hall 331)
Barye, a striking exponent
of Romanticism in the
realm of sculpture, created
dynamic groups of animals
fighting, bringing out the
passion of the struggle, the
force of predatory instincts,
in bold angles of view, ener-
getically modelled forms
and powerful relief surfaces.

Eugène Delacroix (1798–1863)
A Moroccan Saddling a Horse. 1855
Oil on canvas. 56 x 47 cm. (Hall 331)
The East always stirred Delacroix's imagination with its exoticism, colourfulness and incomprehensible passions. Yet the painter strove to subordinate fantasy and the "inspired fury" of execution to the truth of the real world. He spoke of nature being the artist's "dictionary". Back in his youth, in the 1820s, he produced an engraving close in conception and composition to this painting that was entitled *A Turk Saddling a Horse*. It was only the impressions acquired during his trip to Algeria and Morocco in 1832, however, that enabled him to embody the idea in colour, creating a vivid dramatic resonance. Freedom and force of chromatic expressiveness, Delacroix's discoveries in the realm of colour became a source for the searchings of the following generations of French painters, the Realists and Impressionists.

Emile Auguste Carolus-Duran
(1837–1917). *Portrait of Nadezhda Polovtsova*. 1876. Oil on canvas
206.5 x 124.5 cm (Hall 330)
Nadezhda Polovtsova (1838–1908) was, according to family tradition, the illegitimate daughter of Grand Duke Mikhail Pavlovich. She was brought up by Baron Stieglitz and married Alexander Polovtsov, a member of the State Council. This effective portrait was painted during the artist's stay in St Petersburg. Carolus-Duran, a fashionable portraitist with the European aristocracy and a prominent member of the French Academy, was a prominent exponent of "salon art", a type of art "doomed to success" because it combined calm academicism to which the public was accustomed with the effective use of fashionable innovations.

François Xavier (Franz Xaver) Winterhalter
(1806–1873)
Portrait of Countess Sophia Naryshkina. 1858
Oil on canvas. 150 x 114 cm (Hall 330)
This portrait of Sophia Naryshkina (1823–1877), the wife of a court chamberlain, was painted by one of Europe's finest salon portraitists. After training at the Munich Academy, Winterhalter lived and worked in Paris from 1834, fulfilling numerous commissions first for King Louis-Philippe, then for Napoleon III. He also worked for the rulers of Britain and Prussia, the Russian Emperor and the St Petersburg aristocracy. Almost every palace in the Russian capital contained portraits by him and many found their way into the Hermitage after the revolution.

84

Jean-Léon Gérome (1824–1904)
The Sale of a Slave Girl
Oil on canvas. 92 x 74 cm
(Hall 330)
This painting's fascinating subject, smoothness, thoroughness and undoubtedly masterly execution ensured one more success for the noted academic painter Gérome at the 1884 Salon. The work was purchased by Grand Duke Ser- gei Alexandrovich who presented it to his wife. The effective works of salon painting in the Hermitage display vividly demonstrate the background of the official aesthetic against which the struggle for the regeneration of art took place. That struggle was waged back at the beginning of the century by the Romantics and they were followed by the Realists and then the Impressionists.

Hypolite Delaroche
(1797–1856)
*Cromwell by the Coffin
of Charles I.* 1849
Oil on canvas
226 x 291 cm (Hall 325)
Like many Romantics striving to bring painting closer to the feelings of his contemporaries, Delaroche simply replaced a Classical subject with a moving episode from more recent history.

Narcisse Diaz de la Peña
(1808–1876). *Gypsies
Listening to the Predictions
of a Young Fortune-Teller*
1848. Oil on canvas
104 x 78 cm (Hall 321)
In tackling Romantic subjects, Diaz de la Peña strove after expressiveness in the manner of painting, in colour and form. His efforts proved closely akin to the searchings of the landscape artists of the Barbizon school whom he joined in the early 1850s.

Théodore Rousseau (1812–1867)
A Market in Normandy. 1832(?)
Oil on canvas. 29.5 x 38 cm (Hall 322)
Théodore Rousseau was one of the main
exponents of the French Realist landscape
and the creator of the Barbizon school.
After a period of making trips there, in the
1850s he settled in the village of Barbizon
near Fontainebleau where he painted landscapes directly from life, *en plein air*. It
was this method that became key for the
Barbizon landscape artists, a group shar-
ing Rousseau's views. This scene, painted,
it is believed, during a trip to Normandy
in 1832, is one of the finest in the Hermitage's collection of Rousseau's works.

Jules Dalou (1838–1902)
A French Peasant Woman
Terracotta. Height: 125 cm (Hall 323)
The Realism that had its origins in the
landscape painting of the Barbizon school
had by the middle of the nineteenth century become a powerful tendency in art to
which the sculptor Dalou also belonged.

Jules Dupré (1811–1889)
Forest Landscape. Early 1840s
Oil on canvas. 39 x 58 cm (Hall 323)
Dupré, a leading member of the Barbizon school, a friend and follower of Théodore Rousseau, painted his *plein-air* landscapes not at Barbizon, but in the forests north of Paris. Dupré loved sunlight — the contrast of hues, colour reflexes on the cold surface of water, golden highlights in the dark foliage and in the damp, dense brown soil.

Charles François Daubigny (1817–1878)
Seashore at Villerville. 1875
Oil on canvas. 85 x 149 cm (Hall 321)
The seashore at Villerville, a small place on the Normandy coast, was a motif to which Daubigny, a member of the Barbizon school, returned several times. The end result of drawings and *plein-air* studies was a monumental canvas in which land, trees, water and sky merge in endless space, wrapped in moist air.

France, 19th–20th Centuries

Constant Troyon
(1810–1865). *Setting Off for Market*. 1859. Oil on canvas. 260.5 x 211 cm (Hall 322)
Troyon is a distinctive member of the Barbizon group. He was a painter of animals who depicted his subjects in a natural setting. Troyon profoundly mastered both the Barbizon school's lessons in *plein-air* painting and the techniques of the Dutch seventeenth-century animal painters (for which he made a special trip to Holland in 1847). He conveys in a vivid, convincing manner the unhurried movement of a herd in the cold morning fog, through which the first rays of the sun are penetrating.

The artists who became leaders of Realist tendency, Gustave Courbet and François Millet, are represented in the Hermitage by only one, not particularly significant painting (Hall 322). All the greater value therefore attaches to the museum's rich collection of Barbizon school landscape to which Realism owes its most important

attainments. The method of working in the open air led right to the threshold of the great discovery made by the following generation of painters — the Impressionists. It is no coincidence that some of them, most notably Claude Monet, acknowledged as their teacher one of the most outstanding landscape artists and one closely connected to the Barbizon school — Camille Corot.

Jean-Baptiste Camille Corot
(1796–1875). *Peasant Woman Pasturing a Cow by the Edge of a Forest*. 1865–70 Oil on canvas. 47.5 x 35 cm (Hall 322)
A rich range of colours, extremely subtle gradations of the silvery-grey hue and new technique of working with small brush-strokes enabled the artist to poetically and thrillingly recreate the world of living nature: foggy air, the trembling of autumn leaves and the alert silence of an overcast day.

Claude Monet
(1840–1926)
*Lady in a Garden
(Saint-Adresse)*. 1867
Oil on canvas. 80 x 99 cm
(Hall 319)
Monet made more decisive
use of the Barbizon painters' method: he painted
his work only in the open
air, without finishing it in
the studio. This early work
was created at Saint-
Adresse near Le Havre. In
it Monet tried to "record"
the colours of nature on
canvas using small brush-
strokes of pure colour just
as he had seen them on that clear summer noon, at the
moment when the garden was entered by his brother's
wife, Jeanne Margarite Lecadre — a lady in a white dress
that is painted in dark and light blue, the colour of the
shadows from the yellow parasol.
The method developed by Manet and his friends came to
be known as Impressionism after the first exhibition of
their works in 1874, which included Monet's painting
Impression: Sunrise.

Claude Monet
(1840–1926)
Haystack at Giverny. 1886
Oil on canvas. 61 x 81 cm
(Hall 319)

France, 19th–20th Centuries

Claude Monet (1840–1926). *Corner of the Garden at Montgeron* 1876–77. Oil on canvas 172 x 193 cm (Hall 319) This *Garden* was painted at the estate of Ernest Hoschede, one of the first admirers of Impressionism, in the autumn of 1876. In it the Impressionist method found its full expression. The immense canvas is filled with tiny patches of colour — autumn sunlight colouring the cold air, dense foliage, water and earth. One chance moment in the life of nature is recorded in all its vibrant colourful richness.

Claude Monet (1840–1926)
Waterloo Bridge (Effect of Fog). 1903
Oil on canvas. 65 x 100 cm (Hall 319)
From the mid-1880s Monet created landscape series depicting one and the same motif under different atmospheric and lighting conditions — the haystack, the field of poppies and so on. His already exceptional eye for colour was sharpened even more by constant work in the open air. He was drawn by the difficult task of conveying colour in overcast weather, in mist and fog. For three years in succession, 1899–1901, he travelled to London, always staying in the same hotel from where he had a view of the Thames and its bridges. The result was a series of landscapes studying the effect of the London fog.

Pierre-Auguste Renoir (1841–1919)
Girl with a Fan. 1881. Oil on canvas
65 x 50 cm (Hall 320)
The model for this painting was probably
Alfonsine Fournaise, the daughter of the
owner of *La Grenouillère*, a small restaurant on the Seine where Renoir often
worked. Having gathered all the scattering
of colour in the large bright patches of
the figure and background, he repeated
them on the open fan, setting down for
ever on the canvas this warm light, the
freshness of youth, the tender dreaminess
and charm of "the girl with the fan".

Pierre-Auguste Renoir (1841–1919)
Portrait of the Actress Jeanne Samary. 1878
Oil on canvas. 174 x 101.5 cm (Hall 320)
Renoir, the creator of the Impressionist
portrait, of captivating images of women,
managed in this depiction of the young
actress to convey all the charm of femininity, tenderness and youth.

Edgar Degas (1834–1917)
Woman Combing Her Hair. 1885
Pastel on cardboard. 53 x 52 cm
(Hall 326)
In contrast to the Impressionists, to
whom he was close, the basis of Degas's
art was drawing. In the 1880s he worked
in pastel, a medium that combined the
qualities of drawing and painting. Musicality of line, beauty of colour and... the banality of the subject, the "chance" nature
of the view, the "divine" body shifted into
a corner, looking away — this combination
of poetry and prose, the artist's delight
and the scepticism of the sober-minded
viewer reflected all the complexity of Degas's perception of the world.

Pierre-Auguste Renoir (1841–1919)
Child with a Whip. 1885. Oil on canvas. 105 x 75 cm (Hall 320)
The sandy path, foliage and figure of the child seem to have been woven from the rainbow reflections of sunlight. This may be a portrait of the son of Senator Goujon, a companion to the portrait of his sister now in the National Gallery, Washington. The patches of colour in the figure of the child have been gathered into solid surfaces, into distinct forms. Time and movement have stopped and it is not a chance mood, but the subtly sensed essence of childhood, of the character of the child, that comes across in the appearance of the youngster. Thus, in the mid-1880s Renoir was attempting to go beyond the bounds of the Impressionist method, to bring drawing back into painting and with it the depth and multifaceted quality of the painterly image.

Camille Pissarro
(1830–1903)
*The Boulevard
Montmartre in Paris.* 1897
Oil on canvas. 73 x 92 cm
(Hall 318)
One of the main themes in
the work of the Impressionist Pissarro was the life of
the modern city. In the late
1890s he regularly came to
Paris and produced a series
of cityscapes. His views of
the Boulevard Montmartre
were painted from a win-
dow of the Hôtel de Roussy.
While recreating in colour
the semitransparent air of
spring, Pissarro does not
dissolve forms in it: the per-
spective of the street, the
masses of the buildings, the
trees, the carriages and the
noisy crowd retain their
uniqueness in the canvas.
This is Paris as seen through
the eyes of Pissarro in early
spring 1897.

Alfred Sisley (1839–1899)
*The Town of Villeneuve-la-Garenne on the
Banks of the Seine.* 1872. Oil on canvas
59 x 80.5 cm (Hall 319)
English-born Sisley, who participated in
the struggle for Impressionism with Renoir,
Monet and Pissarro from the outset, travelled the hard road of the rejected artist to
the end. But this painting, that probably
hung in the first Impressionist exhibition
of 1874, is full of light, joy and the subtle
lyricism that marked Sisley's painting.

Paul Cézanne (1839–1906)
The Smoker. Circa 1890–92
Oil on canvas. 92.5 x 73.5 cm (Hall 318)
Cézanne is one of the great figures of
Post-Impressionism. That brief period in
the history of French art in the last years
of the nineteenth century threw up a
whole constellation of talents, of great
loners. They were united by one thing —
all of them drew upon Impressionism;
they began with it and went further along
their own way. Cézanne's *Smoker* is a Prov-
ençal peasant, seemingly fashioned from
the same material as the landscape of the
artist's native Provence — of patches and
surfaces of paint as hot as the earth and
the sun of the South and as cols as mountain air and water. This late work, relating
to the artist's series of smokers and card-
players, was created in the early 1890s.

Paul Cézanne
(1839–1906)
Self-Portrait in a Cap
1873–75. Oil on canvas
53 x 39.7 cm (Hall 318)
In the 1870s Cézanne
mastered Impression-
ism, working *en plein
air* at Auvers and Pon-
toise. The self-portrait
from those difficult
years recorded a face
with a ardent gaze,
traces of early ageing,
spiritual turmoils and
loneliness.

Paul Cézanne (1839–1906)
*Girl at the Piano
(The Tannhauser Overture)*
Circa 1868–69
Oil on canvas. 57 x 92 cm
(Hall 318)
This is one of the rare early
works by Cézanne, painted
during the years when he
was closely linked to the
future Impressionists and
living between his native
Aix-en-Provence and Paris.
Depicting a room in his
father's house, his mother
and sister at the piano, he
subordinates the abstracted colour surfaces of the
space, the figures and the
objects to a heavy rhythm
that is not devoid of sol-
emn gloom, a rhythm that
does indeed resemble that
of Wagner's music. In this
painting the might of Cé-
zanne's constructive vi-
sion, his sense of the beauty of form and space, was
already emerging.

Paul Cézanne (1839–1906)
The Great Pine-Tree near Aix. Late 1890s
Oil on canvas. 72 x 91 cm (Hall 318)
This is one of the Cézanne masterpieces in a Hermitage collection of eleven of his works. The majority of them were painted in Provence to which the artist returned permanently in 1886 and where he created his most powerful and profound works. A pine-tree outside Aix with mighty branches, trunk and needles, heated by a hot sun and not fitting within the space of the painting, comes across here as the very embodiment of life itself that is feeding the roots in the warm earth, pulsating with sap beneath the bark and bubbling over in the lush greenery.

Paul Cézanne (1839–1906). *Mont Sainte-Victoire.* 1900
Oil on canvas. 78 x 99 cm (Hall 318)
Mont Sainte-Victoire in Provence is one of the favourite motifs of Cézanne's late landscapes. He spent his life at the foot of this mountain. It appears here lit by the noon-day sun. Life is pulsing at its base, but it reigns above it, as always, remote, cold, surging towards the glowing heavens, towering in its calm majesty over the busy world of the valleys.

Paul Cézanne (1839–1906)
Still Life with Drapery
Circa 1899. Oil on canvas
53 x 72 cm (Hall 318)
This still life, one of Cézanne's best, was painted
in the late 1890s during
one of his then-rare visits
to Paris. In these simple
objects — the firm fruit,
heavy with vital juices, the
gleam and resonance of the
porcelain jug and the luxury
of heavy fabric — we can
sense the mighty energy of
life, the strength and passion of an artist. struggling
over the secret of existence,
and the great power of Cézanne's painting.

Paul Cézanne (1839–1906). *The Banks of the Marne.* 1888
Oil on canvas. 65 x 81 cm (Hall 318)
This is a mature work by the artist reflecting his many-
facetted perception of the world. In the character of the
brushstroke, its form and positioning on the canvas, in
colour and in tone, Cézanne is seeking what is appropri-
ate to the material qualities of nature. His painting itself
becomes the lazy flow of cool river water, the lush vigour
of the bushes, the slenderness of the cypresses and the
white wall of the house warmed by the sun.

Henri "Douanier" Rousseau (1844–1910)
*In the Tropical Forest. Struggle between
a Tiger and a Buffalo.* 1908
Oil on canvas. 46 x 55 cm. (Hall 317)
Rousseau was one of the most striking representatives of a tendency that arose around the turn of the twentieth century in various parts of Europe — art produced by unprofessional, self-taught artists. He spent all his life working in the civil service, chiefly as a tax collector in the Paris toll office, and devoted himself entirely to painting only in retirement. The scene of a clash between wild animals in a jungle was suggested to Rousseau by an etching published in a magazine as well as his visits to the zoo. Perhaps it was precisely his lack of professional training that helped him to retain a freshness of imagination and almost childish naivety and immediacy of artistic expression.

Paul Signac (1863–1935)
The Harbour in Marseilles. 1906
Oil on canvas. 46 x 55 cm. (Hall 317)
This, the only painting by Signac in the Hermitage, together with a work by Henri Edmond Cross (also Hall 317) gives an idea of the Neo-Impressionism created by Georges Seurat who is not himself represented in the museum. Following on from the Impressionists, the Neo-Impressionists divided colour into pure patches and chromatic zones (they often called their method "Divisionism"), applying their paints in tiny dots (hence the more common name "Pointillism" from *point* meaning "dot").

Vincent van Gogh (1853–1890). *Lilac Bush.* 1889
Oil on canvas. 72 x 92 cm (Hall 317)
Lilac Bush was painted in May 1889 in the garden of the
sanatorium at Saint-Rémy near Arles after Van Gogh's first
attack of the serious psychological disorder brought on by
loneliness, poverty and fanatical dedication to his work.
Barely over the attack, van Gogh again took up the brush
and created this masterpiece. Dishevelled, ragged, stirred
by the sun, the wind, by life, surging into the cold, impene-
trable blue of the sky, the bush becomes a symbol of abid-
ing hope, of an unquenched thirst for life.

Vincent van Gogh
(1853–1890)
*Ladies of Arles. Memories
of the Garden at Etten.* 1888
Oil on canvas. 73 x 92 cm
(Hall 317)
Three of the four paintings
in the Hermitage by the
great Dutchman Van Gogh
were produced in the
south of France, at Arles,
where the artist lived for
the last two years of his
short life and where his
talent reached its highest
peak. The beauty of southern nature and memories
of the garden of his par-
ents' house in Holland
became interwoven in this
symbolic image of earth, of
nature with its generous
flowering extolling wom-
an, her labours, her spiritual warmth and all her life.

Paul Gauguin (1848–1903)
Woman Holding a Fruit. 1893
Oil on canvas. 92 x 73 cm (Hall 316)

All the fifteen Gauguins in the Hermitage were painted by the artist in Oceania, where he went in 1891 to produce sketches of nature and life on the island of Tahiti for the French Ministry of Education. There Gauguin experienced moments of the deep intimacy with nature after which he was always striving and this filled his paintings with profound, mysterious meaning. The second title of this painting comes from the words "Where are you going?" written by Gauguin in Kanak, the language of the natives of Tahiti. They use the question as a greeting. Where is this Tahitian Eve so carefully carrying this heavy fruit — the fruit of temptation or the gift of life-producing nature, a symbol of birth and life, its eternal renewal given by Woman.

Paul Gauguin (1848–1903)
Tahitian Pastorals. 1893
Oil on canvas
87.5 x 113.7 cm (Hall 316)
The harmony of life, human, animal and plant — the great and eternal law of existence — that is what Gauguin came to sense so powerfully and profoundly on Tahiti. Coloured surfaces and patches come on unnoticed, in a barely detectable wave, as if flowing one into the other. Everything is subordinated to a mighty and irresistible rhythm. The quiet sounds of the *vivo*, the flute of the ancients, ring out and human being, animal and the natural world comes o a stop, enchanted.

Paul Gauguin (1848–1903)
Sunflowers. 1901
Oil on canvas. 73 x 92 cm (Hall 316)
This is one of Gauguin's last paintings, produced two years before his death on the Oceanic island of St Dominique to which the artist returned in the au-

tumn 1895, having left France forever in the face of disappointments, privations and lack of understanding. The gloomy tones of this painting and its mysterious visual symbols are the expression of the painter's nostalgia for the past, for the life passing away.

101

Auguste Rodin (1840–1917)
The Bronze Age. Sculptor's
model. 1877. Plaster
of Paris. Height: 175 cm
(Hall 318)
This is a model for the celebrated statue that was
Rodin's first major work.
It evoked strong attacks
from both critics and public when shown at the
1878 Salon in Paris. Yet it
was with this piece that
the fame of the great inno-
vator who opened up new
paths for European sculp-
ture began. In his plastic
art Rodin was close to Impressionism, striving to
animate the inert sculptural material with the movement, breath and warmth
of life. *The Bronze Age* is
the quivering thrill of life
roused in a young human
body, the awakening of the
soul, of consciousness at
the dawn of humanity.

Auguste Rodin (1840–1917)
The Poet and the Muse. 1905
Marble. Height: 63 cm
(Hall 318)
The classical theme of poetic inspiration, which was
always expressed allegorically through the muse,
the embodiment of the fe-
male principle, is given immediate, sensual tempera-
mental expression in
Rodin's sculpture. Deliber-
ately unfinished rounded
forms — like unrestrained
patches of colour thrown
onto a canvas — are con-
nected into a single form
by the fast, fluent move-
ment. The poet pressing his
whole body to the muse, is
absorbing the deep-running
energy of the muse's female
energy and accumulating
creative energy.

Auguste Rodin (1840–1917)
Eternal Spring. 1905. Marble. Height: 77 cm
It seems that right before our eyes two powerful, lithe naked bodies emerge from an accidentally cracked piece of marble, draw together and merge in a passionate embrace. It was not, however, the fleeting flow of existence that concerned the sculptor, but its depths. The rock from which the beautiful bodies seem to be born is not a specific image, but some perpetual material without beginning or end. It was not without good cause that Rodin gave this group the symbolic title *Eternal Spring.*

Pierre Bonnard
(1867–1947)
Morning in Paris
1911. Oil on canvas. 76.5 x 122 cm
(Hall 343)

< Pierre Bonnard
(1867–1947)
Evening in Paris
1911. Oil on canvas. 76 x 121 cm
(Hall 343)

Bonnard's oeuvre is represented in the Hermitage by masterpieces from the early period when the artist belonged to the group known as the Nabis, who represented the last tendency in Post-Impressionism. The word Nabi meant a prophet. These exponents of Symbolism were young, but already well known. They sought to produce modern art that was involved with "eternity", infused with spirituality like the great art of the past. In the studio that they called the "Temple", they discussed issues of religion and philosophy, the esoteric doctrines of the East and listened to music. Bonnard, however, was not so much a "prophet" as a talented and subtle painter. *Morning in Paris* and *Evening in Paris* — companion pieces commissioned by the Muscovite collector Ivan Morozov — are not simply street scenes snatched from the flow of existence. The painter transforms the life of Parisian streets and squares into a symphony of colour, a magical enchantment of paints, full of mysteries and things not fully said.

Maurice Denis (1870–1943)
Martha and Mary. 1896
Oil on canvas. 77 x 116 cm
(Hall 343)
Denis, the leader and theo-
retician of the Nabis, one
of the chief creators of the
Art Nouveau style in painting, strove to revive
"sacred art", to translate
classical subjects from mythology and the Gospel
into the contemporary
language of subdued col-
ours, flowing lines and
musical rhythms.

> **Felix Vallotton**
(1865–1925). *Interior.* 1904
Oil on cardboard
61.5 x 56 cm (Hall 343)
The private life of a human
dwelling is transformed in
the works of the Swiss
Nabi Valloton into a skilful
arrangement of colours on
the surface of the canvas.
Balancing in his painting
both objects and the fig-
ures of living people, Valloton emphasizes the deco-

rative nature of the com-
position in which one in-
evitably senses the cool
irony and sober formalism
of an artist who had al-
ready entered the twenti-
eth century.

France, 19th–20th Centuries

Pablo Picasso (1881–1973)
Boy with a Dog. 1905
Gouache on cardboard. 57 x 41 cm
Picasso, a Spaniard who spent almost all his life in France and became one of the twentieth century's greatest artists, is represented in the Hermitage by an exceptionally rich collection of early works. This gouache belongs to his "Pink Period": the boy with a dog comes from the same world of wandering players, circus artistes and clowns that seemed so pure and human to the artist. The shy, golden-pink light that disperses the darkness and brings back hope seems to proceed from the pair themselves; lonely and unfortunate, they give warmth to one another.

Pablo Picasso (1881–1973)
The Absinthe Drinker. 1901
Oil on canvas. 73 x 54 cm (Hall 348)
This work belongs to the "Blue Period" that covered Picasso's first years in Paris. He quickly became the most prominent figure in the French capital's artistic avant-garde. Here he interprets a subject that had earlier attracted Toulouse-Lautrec in his own way: he reduces the colourful variety of a Montmartre café to a gloomy, cold blue tone with a Spanish severity about it. The lapidary nature of composition and line, and the bold deformation in the depiction of the female figure, locked in her own embrace and pressed mercilessly into the corner, heightens the dramatic intensity of the image.

< **Pablo Picasso** (1881–1973). *The Visit (Two Sisters).* 1902
Oil on canvas pasted onto panel. 152 x 100 cm (Hall 348)
This is one of the most significant works from the Blue Period in which Picasso attained extreme asceticism and tragic tension in the colour blue. Using this dull, heavy chromatic material the painter constructs two pillar-like female figures resisting the pressing force of dark vaults. The literary subject, the meeting in prison of two sisters, a nun and a prostitute, takes on the character of painted metaphor full of significance.

Pablo Picasso (1881–1973)
Musical Instruments. 1912
Oil on canvas. 98 x 80 cm
(Hall 349)
This work is an example of late Cubism. Random fragments of objects, created in colour or from pieces of wallpaper, sand and sawdust, using the collage technique that Picasso invented, are united by the tensely vibrating rhythm to become a new, associative, metaphorical reality. The world is pared down to a tight space confined within the oval and filled with the restrained passionate thrum of Spanish guitars.

> **Pablo Picasso**
(1881–1973)
*Woman with a Fan
(After the Ball).* 1908
Oil on canvas
152 x 101 cm
This is one of Picasso's most famous Cubist works. Here he does not tell a story or describe the forms visible to the eye, but reveals their simple and crude constructional essence, brining out in the abstracted geometrical structures some unchanging painted-constructed type of the tragic and lonely *Woman with a Fan.*

Pablo Picasso (1881–1973)
Green Bowl and Black Bottle
1908. Oil on canvas
61 x 51 cm
Picasso's interest in the still life awoke with the shift to the Cubist method that began in 1907. Laying absolutely bare the inner structure of simple objects, Picasso attains a sensation of some sort of intrinsic, secret truth of things.

Henri Matisse (1869–1954). *Music*. 1910
Oil on canvas. 260 x 389 cm (Hall 344)
Between a blue sky and a green hill a group whirls round holding hands, their naked bodies flying in a headlong rhythm are splashed across the canvas, glowing red — the hot colour of passion and of life. But suddenly, in the other gigantic canvas, the hands have separated, the ring has become still. The red patches of the bodies thrust into the blue. Compressed like springs they burn against the green with unendurable fire and it emanates from the black spots of the mouths in monotonous tones that are accompanied by long notes on the pipes and the scraping of the violin.

Henri Matisse (1869–1954)
The Dance. 1910. Oil on canvas. 270 x 391 cm (Hall 344)

The Hermitage possesses 37 paintings by Matisse. They all date from his period of intense artistic searching, the time of the first avant-garde movement of the twentieth century, Fauvism, of which Matisse was the head, and of the individual system of painting that the great artist based upon it.

The Dance and *Music* are a pair of decorative panels that Matisse painted for the Moscow mansion of the collector of modern art Sergei Shchukin. They are an astonishingly simple, majestic, large-scale, sensual and visible expression of the idea of human creativity.

Henri Matisse (1869–1954)
The Red Room (Dessert. Harmony in Red). 1908
Oil on canvas. 180 x 220 cm (Hall 344)
The leading role in this programmatic work by Matisse is played by the colour red. It fills almost the entire canvas, dominating all its shades. Chromatic harmony here is not a characteristic of an attractive interior, it is an artistic sign of beauty, it is beauty itself, but not abstract and formal, but associated with the warm, living world of daily human existence.

Henri Matisse (1869–1954)
The Artist's Family. 1911
Oil on canvas. 143 x 194 cm (Hall 345)
The idea for this portrait came from Shchukin, the first and greatest buyer and commissioner of Matisse's paintings. Under the influence of Islamic art, with which he became acquainted at an exhibition in Paris, Matisse when depicting his own wife, sons and daughter linked them with a patternwork of Oriental ornament.

Henri Matisse (1869–1954)
Still Life with a Blue Tablecloth. 1909
Oil on canvas. 88 x 118 cm (Hall 345)
This blue tablecloth was kept in Matisse's studio and featured in several of his paintings. In projecting it onto the flat surface of the canvas, the artist almost stripped it of its material quality, leaving only the azure colour and the broad arabesques of the pattern as a sign of pure beauty free of banal utility.

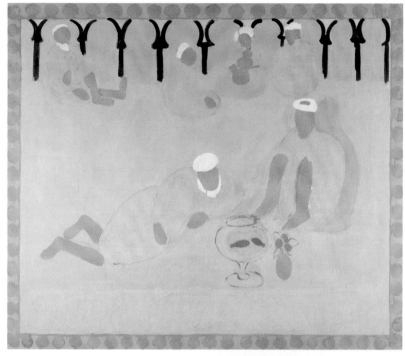

Henri Matisse (1869–1954)
Arab Coffee House. 1913
Oil on canvas. 176 x 210 cm (Hall 345)
In 1912 and 1913 Matisse made two trips
to Morocco that, as he himself admitted,
helped him to gain new links with the
world he depicted. *Arab Coffee House* is one
of the best works of his Moroccan cycle.
Matisse does not imitate the East, is not
carried away by its exoticism, but rather
tries to penetrate it with his soul. Dissolving the faceless patches of the figures in
a semitransparent grey-blue colour, as if
they were swimming in water behind the
thick glass of an aquarium, he makes us
sense a state of complete detachment from
the hustle and bustle of life, a shift into
some sort of non-existence, nirvana.

Henri Matisse (1869–1954)
Moroccan Woman (Zorah). 1912
Oil on canvas. 146 x 61 cm (Hall 345)
The Moroccan Zorah, an embodiment
of the refinement of the East, was a favourite model for Matisse. She appears in
a number of his paintings and drawings.

Henri Matisse (1869–1954)
Conversation. 1909
Oil on canvas. 177 x 217 cm (Hall 345)
The personages of this painting are Matisse and his wife Amélie. The Conversation is taking place between them. Yet the painting has nothing of the genre scene about it. It is majestic and monumental as some ancient fresco. The true hero of the painting is the colour blue. It is a sign of the shadow from which the man and woman appeared and within which they conduct their tense dialogue; a sign of the mystery of their eternal confrontation and connection. The indivisibility of that link is emphasized by the black grille cast between the man and woman, while the tree-trunk and greenery outside the window are a symbol and sign of life that has emerged from the shadow and is warmed by the sum. Thus colour takes on a deep symbolic meaning in Matisse's painting.

Henri Matisse (1869–1954)
Portrait of Lydia Delectorskaya. 1947
Oil on canvas. 64.5 x 49.5 cm (Hall 345)
The Russian émigré Lydia Delectorskaya was Matisse's secretary for many years, right up to the artist's death. She was a model for many of his paintings and drawings. She presented this portrait to the Hermitage in 1967, together with a number of other works by the artist.

Maurice de Vlaminck (1876–1958)
View of the Seine. Circa 1905–06
Oil on canvas. 54.5 x 65.5 cm (Hall 346)
Vlaminck was one of the main exponents
of Fauvism, a tendency that was itself short-
lived (late 1890s–1907), but had a tremendous influence on twentieth-century art.
Its main feature was the unrestrained use
of colour, that led to the use of the word
"fauves" — "wild beasts" to describe the
group of artists. Pure colours boldly applied
to the canvas and unconnected by drawing,
powerful contrasts and complex textures
give Fauvist works an almost glaring vividness and a fascinating expressivity.

Fernand Léger (1881–1955)
Carte Postale. Oil on canvas. 92 x 65 cm
(Hall 350)
This painting by a classic twentieth-century
figure, a painter, graphic artist and creator of
monumental compositions was presented by
a group of his pupils in 1949. Leger's main
theme was an assertion of the beauty of the
new reality created by the engineering and
technical thinking of the twentieth century
in unity with the world of living nature.

114

France, 19th–20th Centuries

Georges Rouault (1871–1958)
Spring. Watercolour and pastel
on cardboard. 60 x 57 cm (Hall 326)
One of the Fauves, Rouault would always
retain a passion for the expressivity of
colour, a powerful means of conveying
the artist's tragic perception of the world.

André Derain (1880–1954)
*Portrait of an Unknown Man Reading a
Newspaper (Chevalier X).* 1914
Oil on canvas. 162.5 x 97.5 cm (Hall 347)
The name *Chevalier X* was given to this
painting by Guillaume Apollinaire who
shared and supported the ideas of Cubism.

André Derain (1880–1954)
The Grove. 1912. Oil on canvas
116 x 81 cm (Hall 347)
Derain, one of the original Fauves, shifted
towards Cubism after 1908. The new movement proved congenial to his constructional perception of nature and objects, his
purely Gallic passion for logic and clarity
of expression. The trees in his *Grove* are
constructed from almost single-coloured
dense material divided up into hard facets
of light and dark. From them he formed
the springy volumes of the soil, the mighty
trunks, the branches and the rounded
crowns. In their strict alternation and re-
lentlessly persistent introduction into the
space one can sense the creative force of a
mysterious, mighty reason that makes and
organizes the world of living nature.

Albert Marquet
(1875–1947)
Marina (Naples). 1909
Oil on canvas. 61.5x 80 cm
(Hall 350)
On the basis of Fauvism
Marquet developed a free
and assured manner of
painting. A few precise
touches of the brush pro-
duce, as if spontaneously,
the glistening waters
of the Bay of Naples.

Raoul Dufy (1877–1953)
*Regatta (Sailing Ships
in the Harbour of Deauville)*
Circa 1936. Oil on canvas
54 x 80.8 cm (Hall 350)
The Fauvism that this artist pursued early in his
career became trans-
formed in Dufy's mature
years into a gentle, lyrical
expressionism.

Chaim Soutine
(1893–1944)
Self-Portrait with a Beard
1916. Oil on canvas
54 x 30.5 cm (Hall 350)
This work by the noted
Expressionist artist, a Jew
of Russian-Lithuanian origin who lived in France,
was purchased in 1998.

Kees van Dongen (1877–1968)
Lady in a Black Hat. Circa 1908
Oil on canvas. 100 x 81.5 cm
(Hall 347)
The artistic bohemia of Montmartre, an artificial world of glaring colours, bold and wickedly alluring beautiful women — that was the theme of the Fauvism of Dutch-born Kees van Dongen. It seems that the artist is fascinated only with the superficial glamour of that life, reflected in his painting in the exaggeratedly vivid colour. Yet it was Van Dongen who stated: "A painting should be something that glorifies life and excites, because at heart life is sad and gloomy." The boldness of his painting seems the essence of his model: the black hat, the green shawl and between them the challengingly haughty face of the *femme fatale*.

Germany and Italy, 19th–20th Centuries

Department of Western European Art

The halls overlooking the courtyard on the second floor of the Winter Palace house nineteenth- and twentieth-century sculpture and painting. Besides the fairly well known collections of German and Italian sculpture, there are also individual works by Belgian, Dutch, Swiss, Finnish, Spanish, American and Canadian sculptors of this period.

█ FRANCE: 19TH–20TH CENTURIES

█ GERMANY, ITALY AND OTHER EUROPEAN
COUNTRIES: 19TH–20TH CENTURIES

❷ COMMANDANT'S STAIRCASE (ACCESS TO
THE GROUNDFLOOR AND THE FIRST FLOOR)

❸ WOODEN STAIRCASE (ACCESS
TO THE FIRST FLOOR)

SECOND FLOOR

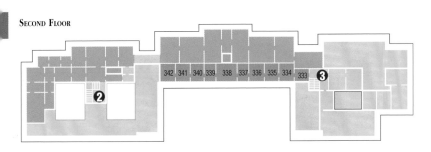

The capital of European art in the nineteenth century was Paris, so much so that the names and achievements of artists working elsewhere in Europe during this period were, with rare exceptions, known only in their homelands. The situation that prevailed in the fine arts through the nineteenth century began to change at the beginning of the twentieth, when avant-garde artistic tendencies emerged in Germany and Italy, promoting those countries to leading centres of modern culture. Italian Futurism and German Expressionism became an important component link in the art of the new century.

The Hermitage's collection of German nineteenth-century painting is, despite its fairly small size, today considered the finest outside Germany. The majority of works come from the collections of the Duke of Leuchtenberg (who married a daughter of Nicholas I) and Count Kushelev-Bezborodko. Sadly, the stocks of twentieth-century German art do not include works by leading Expressionists.

The collection of Italian art is made up for the most part of chance acquisitions. They include two paintings by one of the best Italian artists of the twentieth century, Giorgio Morandi.

118

Friedrich Overbeck (1789–1869)
The Triumph of Religion in Art
Reduced-size replica of a painting
of the same name (1830s–40s)
Oil on canvas. 145 x 146 cm
(Hall 342)
In 1837–38 Tsesarevich Alexander (the
future Alexander II) travelled with his
mentor, the poet Vasily Zhukovsky, around
the major cities of Europe. In Rome they
called on Friedrich Overbeck, the founder
of the group known as the Nazarenes. This
German artist dreamt of reviving the
monumental religious style in art and was
working in his studio on the programmatic painting *The Triumph of Religion in Art*.
Captivated by the artist's talent and the
lofty ideological concept of his work, Zhukovsky commissioned for the heir to the
throne a reduced-size monochrome replica of the work. This was delivered to St
Petersburg a few years later and was given
a place of honour in the private apartments of the future emperor.

Karl Friedrich Lessing (1808–1880)
*The Royal Couple Mourning the Death
of Their Daughter.* 1830. Oil on canvas
215 x 193 cm. (Hall 342)
Lessing was a prominent member of the
Düsseldorf school. He painted this depiction of a king and queen at the age of
twenty-two. The subject would seem to
have been inspired by Ludwig Uhland's
Romantic poem *The Castle by the Sea* that
tells of the sorrow of parents who have
lost their only daughter.

119

Caspar David Friedrich (1774–1840)
The Giant Mountains. Oil on canvas
73.5 x 102.5 cm (Hall 342)
The Hermitage possesses nine works by
Caspar David Friedrich, two of them landscapes. The German Romantics considered
nature to be an archetype of freedom and
of the manifestation of elemental forces
without which true creation was impossi-
ble. Friedrich turned the landscape into a
"field of study" of his own feelings and
spiritual impulses. In his works the life of
nature and the life of the soul, the mood
of the atmosphere and the mood of the
individual are made equivalent to each
other, fused into a single whole.

Caspar David Friedrich (1774–1840)
Night in the Harbour (Sisters). Circa 1820
Oil on canvas. 74 x 52 cm (Hall 342)
Night in the Harbour is a typical composition by this great Romantic painter in which
real-life details are fantastically interwoven
with imaginary ones underlining the supposed authenticity of the scene. The two
women, depicted with their backs to us, are
absorbed in silent contemplation of the
night-time harbour. Straight in front of
them rises a monument to lost sailors —
a large cross and anchor — an important
element for the meaning of the painting.

Caspar David Friedrich (1774–1840)
On a Sailing Ship. 1818–19
Oil on canvas. 71 x 56 cm (Hall 342)
On a Sailing Ship, a Romanticized reflection of a real-life event — something extremely rare in Friedrich's work, was acquired by the future Nicholas I in the artist's studio in 1820. It found a home in the personal apartments of his young wife, Alexandra Fiodorovna, who had been Princess Louise Charlotte of Prussia before their marriage in 1817.

This canvas was painted immediately after Friedrich's honeymoon trip with his bride Caroline to the island of Rügen, off the German Baltic coast As a whole the work has a metaphorical meaning. It is more poetic dream than reality, symbolizing the voyage together of two lovers through the "sea of life", their striving towards a bright goal.

Ludwig Knaus
(1829–1910)
Girl in a Field. 1857
Oil on canvas. 50 x 59 cm
(Hall 341)
In Russia Ludwig Knaus was one of the most popular artists belonging to the Düsseldorf school of the second half of the nineteenth century. In the 1850s he lived in Paris, where he was taken by the work of the Barbizon school painters, but the greatest impression on him was made by the painting of the great French Realist Gustave Courbet.

Hans von Marees (1837–1887)
Courtyard with a Grotto in the Royal Residence in Munich. Oil on canvas
240 x 162 cm (Hall 341)
Marees was a celebrated German Symbolist, the creator of monumental canvases on allegorical themes. *Courtyard with a Grotto* differs from the artist's other works in style and quality of execution. The figure of the lady seems to have been taken from one of the "Small Dutch Masters". The peacock, fountain and section of the palace wall could be part of a Renaissance work. The artist produced this work to commission, to adorn Baron Stieglitz's mansion in St Petersburg.

Anselm Feuerbach (1829–1880)
Self-Portrait. Oil on canvas
92 x 73 cm (Hall 341)
Feuerbach is known for his monumental works on themes from German epic poetry that adorned the palaces of patrons of the arts and public buildings. This self-portrait was apparently painted at Karlsruhe, where the artist settled after his return from Paris. He was fond of shocking the provincial public, strolling around town in a red cape and top-hat.

Franz von Stuck (1863–1928)
Fight over a Woman. 1905
Oil on panel. 90 x 117 cm (Hall 339)
Franz von Stuck was a leading representative of German Symbolism, the founder of the Munich "Sezession" and a gifted teacher at the Academy of Arts, from whose studio many major figures of the twentieth century emerged, including Wassily Kandinsky. *Fight over a Woman* is a typical popular subject from the turn of the century, reflecting the philosopher Nietzsche's beloved idea of the cult of the superman — a powerful individual overcoming the resistance of the bourgeois conventions of society by brute, animal force.

Heinrich Campendonck (1889–1957)
Man and Animals among Nature
Oil on canvas. 95 x 65 cm (Hall 338)
In 1911 joined the ranks of the *Blauer Reiter* group that Kandinsky had organized in Munich. This association, together with the *Brücke* group, became the foundation of Expressionism in German art in the early twentieth century. After the First World War Expressionist ideas no longer interested the German public. Campendonck withdrew to a remote village and completely gave up participating in exhibitions.

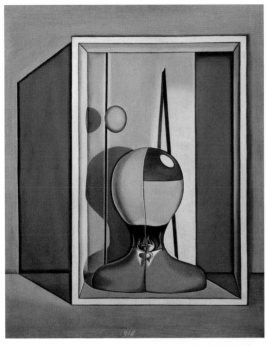

Giorgio Morandi
(1890–1964)
Metaphysical Still Life. 1918
Oil on canvas. 71.5 x 61.5 cm
(Hall 337)
Morandi was one of the most significant and popular Italian artists of the twentieth century. He worked mainly in the still-life genre. *Metaphysical Still Life* dates from the time of Morandi's absorption with the work of Giorgio de Chirico who produced a new metaphysical theory of painting that asserted that an artist's creation should reflect only those images that he draws from the depths of the subconscious. Emphatically three-dimensional objects casting shadows so sharp they look like they have been drawn with a draughtsman's instruments are placed in an enclosed, airless space and look unusual and mysterious.

Giorgio Morandi
(1890–1964)
Still Life. 1920s. Oil on canvas. 51 x 57.5 cm
(Hall 337)
Morandi was born and spent all his life in Bologna, a city that in the early twentieth century became one of the centres of new Italian art. He received a classical education at the Bologna Academy of Arts, but already in his youth he became fascinated by the work of Paul Cézanne and other innovative French artists of the late nineteenth century. In the refined, expressive still lifes of his mature period one can sense the influence of Cézanne, and also of Classical painting from the seventeenth and eighteenth centuries.

Germany and Italy, 19th–20th Centuries

Massimo Campigli (1895–1971)
Seamstresses. 1925. Oil on canvas
161 x 96.5 cm. (Hall 337)
Campigli was a journalist and writer with no special artistic training. While living in Paris, he became taken with modern art and was particularly interested by the Cubism practised by Picasso and Léger. On becoming an artist himself, Campigli sought to reinvigorate the traditions of monumental art, combining avant-garde experimentation with a profound study of the art of great masters of the past — from paintings on Etruscan sarcophagi to the frescoes of Giotto, Masaccio and Piero della Francesca.

Renato Guttuso
(1912–1987)
Portrait of Rocco and His Son. 1960. Oil on canvas. 136 x 113 cm (Hall 337)
Guttuso was a prominent Italian artist of the middle years of the twentieth century, the creator and leader of Neo-Realism, the foremost trend in Italian painting in the 1950s. This artist's painting is filled with expression. He was not afraid to bring crashing together bright, contrasting shades of colour and boldly distorted form in order to achieve the maximum eloquence in an image. Rocco, the artist's assistant and friend, was for Guttuso the embodiment of the Italian national character.

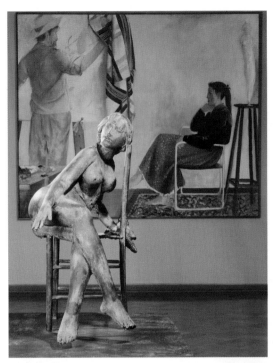

Giacomo Manzu
(1908–1990)
Tebe Sitting. 1983
Bronze. Height: 125 cm
(Hall 337)
Three bronze statues, reliefs and the painting *Artist and Model* were presented to the Hermitage in 1986 by the sculptor Giacomo Manzu, one of the leading exponents of Italian Realism. Together they give a fairly complete impression of the style of this notable figure of the century just past. In the 1980s Manzu often produced works in which a nude female figure was placed on a broad, low plinth, creating the illusion of a picture frame. The dynamics of the figure's movement emphasize her unstable pose — the model's body seems balanced on the edge of the seat that is also included in the overall composition.

Giacomo Manzu (1908–1990)
Crucifixion. Relief. Bronze. 68.5 x 49.5
(Hall 336)
In the 1930s Mazu worked in a technique known as "low relief", where the design is almost a drawing, barely protruding from the surface of the bronze. The artist gave his works an almost "painting-like" resonance in which the glints of light seem like dabs of colour. The theme of the Crucifixion that Manzu pursued in this period expressed itself in a series of reliefs where tradition combines with modernity, beauty with ugliness, the ideal with the coarse, almost grotesque.

>> **Emilio Greco** (1911–1995)
Large Seated Nude. 1969
Bronze. H 133 cm (Hall 335)
Emilio Greco was a monumental sculptor whose works adorn towns in Italy and further afield. A variant of *Large Seated Nude* stands on one of the central squares in London. The Hermitage has twenty of the artist's works donated after exhibition here.

Francesco Messina (1900–1995)
Beatrice. 1959. Bronze. H 145 cm (Hall 335)
Francesco Messina was one of the prominent exponents of the realistic tendency in
Italian sculpture. Veneration for the masterpieces of Antiquity and the Renaissance
combines in this artist's work with a love
of real-life models. The Hermitage possesses twenty works by Messina, donated by
the sculptor after an exhibition in 1981.

Augusto Murer (1923–1991)
Faun. 1980. Bronze. H 195 cm. (Hall 335)
Murer worked mainly in northern Italy,
in Venice where his work is well known.
He created monuments dedicated to the
struggle against Fascism. The Hermitage
has six works by the artist given by him to
the museum after the exhibition in 1981.

Wassily Kandinsky
(1866–1944)
Landscape. 1913
Oil on canvas. 88 x 100 cm
(Hall 334)
The real-life impression is
still present in this colourful
abstract improvization on
the theme of a winter landscape. The range of colours
here is like a powerful musical chord. According to the
artist's theory, shades of
colour can be expressed by
musical sounds: yellow is
close to the sound of the
violin, blue to the cello and
purple or violet to the
double-bass.

Wassily Kandinsky
(1866–1944)
View in Murnau. 1908
Oil on canvas. 33 x 44 cm
(Hall 334)
In 1902 Kandinsky left Russia for Munich. The village
of Murnau, on the edge of
the Alps, is one of the most
picturesque spots in Ger-
many and has long attracted artists. Here Kandinsky
painted a landscape in
which he displayed his brilliant talent as a colourist.

Wassily Kandinsky
(1866–1944). *Winter.* 1909
Oil on canvas. 70 x 97 cm
(Hall 334)
Winter, created at Murnau
in 1909, is evidence of the
artist's gradual shift towards
ever-increasing generaliza-
tion and abstraction of natural forms. Here the objects
seem to be flat patches of
colour, although Kandinsky
does not yet break with
real-life impressions —
the vertical rhythms of the
black lines are a reminder
of the dark trunks of trees
standing out clearly against
the the snow-covered hills.

Wassily Kandinsky
(1866–1944)
Composition No 6. 1913
Oil on canvas. 194 x 294 cm
(Hall 334)
Kandinsky was among the leading figures in twentieth-century art, one of the creators of Abstractionism. The artist himself divided his abstract works into "improvizations", impressions brought by perceptions of the world, and the monumental "compositions" to which he attributed special significance, completely expressing his artistic conception in them. *Composition No 6* is one of the best works of its kind.

Kazimir Malevich (1878–1935)
Black Square. 1929–30(?)
Oil on canvas. 53.5 x 53.5 cm. (Hall 334)
The *Black Square* is one of the chief symbols of the Russian and worldwide avant-garde in the twentieth century. Today four variants of the it are known. The first (now in the Tretyakov Gallery) was painted in 1915. It became the material embodiment of the theory of Suprematism that Malevich created and which, according to him, put an end to "the art of repetition" and opened the way to "the creation of intuitive intelligence". The black square on a white background is a sign, a primary element in Malevich's Suprematist system and so the artist returned constantly to the image over a decade and a half. Yet in doing so, Malevich never copied his first version.

The Department of the History of Russian Culture

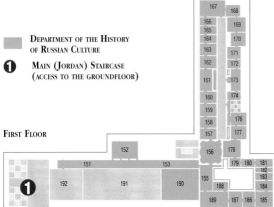

More than thirty second-storey halls on the west side of the Winter Palace are given over to the displays of the Department of the History of Russian Culture. They are housed in rooms that belonged to the Great Imperial Apartment and the grand-ducal apartments.

The halls along the dark corridor (168–174), where Grand Duke Alexander Pavlovich, the future Alexander I, lived at the end of the eighteenth century, were redecorated by Alexander Briullov in the 1830s for the heir to the throne, the future Alexander II, who would die here after the bomb attack of 1 March 1881 (Hall 172). The halls on the other side of the Saltykov Staircase, along the north-western facade of the palace, were occupied successively by Emperors Alexander I, Nicholas I and Nicholas II (Halls 176–189). In the apartment overlooking the courtyard (Halls 157–167) several generations of grand dukes, sons of the Russian emperors, grew up. The displays of this department also occupy some of the palace state rooms (Halls 190–192, 151–156).

The department's extensive stocks, more than 300,000 items spanning a period from the fifth century to the early twentieth, are of a historical and cultural character: an immense collection of works of applied art and crafts, archaeological material and historical documents, works of science and technology, weapons and banners. Russian fine art is represented by a splendid collection of Early Russian icons, eighteenth-century portraits and landscape paintings, and a collection of graphic art. The halls of the Winter Palace – an outstanding architectural and historical monument – are themselves a part of the department. Monuments to the nation's culture existed in the Hermitage even before the revolution: from 1848 to 1910 the Small Hermitage contained the "Cabinet of Peter the Great" with memorial items relating to that Tsar; the Winter Palace had a "museum" of Russian porcelain and silver – the collection of palace tableware. But the Department of the History of Russian Culture was created only in 1941, when the collection of the Russian Museum's Historical and Daily Life Department was transferred to the Hermitage. This consisted of valuables from St Petersburg palaces nationalized after 1917, as well as the collections of noted collectors of antiquities. In recent years the department's stocks have grown considerably and continue to do so thanks to the activities of archaeological and collecting expeditions and purchases by the museum.

St Nicholas of Zaraisk with scenes from his life
First half of the sixteenth century. Tempera on a gessoed panel
165 x 115 cm. Among the items of Early Russian culture from the fifth to the
seventeenth centuries (currently under refurbishment) a special place is
occupied by the rich collection of icons. One of its masterpieces is an image
illustrating the *Tale of Nicholas of Zaraisk* written in the fourteenth century.
That work tells of a Byzantine icon of St Nicholas that came into the possession of Prince Fiodor of Riazan. The Prince was killed by the Tatars, while his
wife to escape their clutches threw herself from a high window. The place
where this happened came to be known as Zaraisk (from an old word meaning "smashed to death") and the icon was called St Nicholas of Zaraisk. The
saint, who was greatly venerated in Russia, is surrounded by 28 marginal
scenes of his life. The icon was brought from the village of Nionoksa in the
White Sea district of Archangelsk region where it was kept in a wooden
church dating from 1727.

Andrei Matveyev
(1704–1739)
Portrait of Peter the Great
After 1725. Copy of Carel
de Moor's original of 1717
Oil on canvas. 78 x 61 cm
(Hall 158)
Matveyev was one of the
first artists of the Russian
school of painting. Peter
sent him and others abroad
on a stipend to study the
basics of European paint-
ing and Matveyev spent
eleven years in Holland.
It was there, when the Tsar
was already dead, that
Matveyev painted this portrait that repeats the composition of his teacher
Carel de Moor, who paint-
ed paired portraits of Peter
and Catherine I in 1717
during the Russian Tsar's
visit to Western Europe.

Alexei Zubov (1683–1751)
Panorama of St Petersburg. 1716
Etching and burin engraving
75.5 x 244.5 cm. (Hall 157)
Engraving was one of the main art forms
in Russia in the first quarter of the eighteenth century as the arts rapidly responded to and reflected the eventful age of
Peter's reforms. St Petersburg, the new
capital of a young Russia founded by the
great reformer, is one of the main subjects
in the work of the celebrated engraver of
the period Alexei Zubov.

The basis of the display of Russian culture of the first quarter of the eighteenth
century (Halls 157–161) was provided by
items from the memorial Cabinet of Peter the Great in the Kunstkammer, supplemented by newer acquisitions. Articles of daily life used by Russian and
foreign craftsmen; the lathes from Peter's
turnery, craft items and products of the
factories Peter founded and personal effects of the Tsar, paintings, sculpture,
engravings, silverware, glass and carved
ivory all come together to form a broad,
vivid panorama of Peter's age.

**The Display of Russian Culture
of the First Quarter of the Eighteenth
Century** (Hall 159)
The hall reproduces the interior of a rich
house in Peter's reign: the painted drop-leaf
table created by craftsmen from Arkhan-
gelsk, an armchair and chairs of European
design, on the wall one of the first Russian
tapestries depicting the Battle of Poltava.

Ship goblet. 1706. St Petersburg
Cast, chased, engraved and gilded silver
30.5 x 12 x 37 cm. (Hall 161)
This goblet was made from the first silver
mined beyond Lake Baikal in honour of a
Russian naval victory on the Baltic.

Copying Lathe. 1729. Andrei Nartov
(1693–1756), St Petersburg
Height: 228.5 cm. (Hall 161)
Peter the Great mastered fourteen crafts.
His favourite was turnery and he kept
a workshop equipped with lathes of the
latest design. Items produced on those
machines can be seen in Hall 162.

Bartolomeo Carlo Rastrelli (1675–1744)
Bust of Peter the Great
1723–29. Bronze
Height: 102 cm. (Hall 158)
The Italian sculptor Bartolomeo Carlo Rastrelli came to Russia in 1716, together with his son, the future famous architect, and lived the rest of his life here. A witness to Peter's reforms, he devoted himself to creating the image of the Tsar in sculpture. This bronze bust of Peter I is Rastrelli's finest work. Depicted in Roman armour and an ermine mantle that seems to be stirred by the Baltic winds, Peter appears the embodiment of determination, energy and vision. On one of the panels decorating the armour, the sculptor depicted the Battle of Poltava, Peter's greatest victory on land, on the other an allegorical composition: Peter as a sculptor carving the figure of a woman who represents the young Russia.

Peter the Great's Campaign Medicine Chest. Circa 1613–15
Augsburg, Germany. Wood, metal and glass with oil painting on copper and gilding. 39.5 x 41 x 32.5 cm
This is one of those personal belongings that Peter always kept with him and that were gathered after his death in 1725 in the memorial Cabinet of Peter the Great. This was located first in the Kunstkammer, then, from 1848 to 1910, in the Hermitage, from where it was moved to the Academy of Sciences. The Cabinet came back to the Hermitage only in 1941. The medicine chest contains many internal drawers with silver plates that contained instruments and equipment for making medicines. The inside of the lid is decorated with a sheet of copper bearing a depiction of an apothecary's shop.

Ivan Vishniakov
(1699–1761)
Portrait of Stepanida Yakovleva. After 1756
Oil on canvas. 90 x 72 cm
(Hall 163)
This wedding portrait and its companion piece, a portrait of the groom who was the son of a prominent St Petersburg merchant, are rare works by Ivan Vishniakov, one of the creators of the Russian school of painting. The portrait is reminiscent of the old *parsuna*, a type of depiction based on the icon, yet at the same time contains much taken from European secular painting: the beauty of the rounded forms is skilfully conveyed as is the gleam of the eyes beneath arching black brows, while the figure itself seems frozen against the dark background.

Ivan Nikitin (1680s–1742). *Portrait of Empress Elizabeth as a Child*. Circa 1712
Oil on canvas. 54 x 43 cm. (Hall 166)
One of the most touching images in early Russian portraiture was painted before the artist went to study in Italy.

Snuffbox with Pugs
1752. The Neva Porcelain Factory of Dmitry Vinogradov (1720(?)–1758), St Petersburg. Porcelain, underglaze painting, mounted with gold
4.7 x 7.6 x 6.2 cm. (Hall 163)
This is one of the earliest examples of Russian porcelain, produced at the Neva Factory founded in St Petersburg by Empress Elizabeth. This became possible after Vinogradov discovered how to produce porcelain paste and laid the foundation of porcelain manufacture in Russia. This snuffbox which he made and had painted by the craftsman A.I. Cherny, was presented to the Empress.

135

Mikhail Lomonosov (1711–1765)
Portrait of Peter the Great. 1755–57, from
the original by Johann Gottfried Tannauer
Smalto mosaic on an iron base
89 x 89 cm. (Hall 162)
This is the most significant work produced in Lomonosov's workshop at the
Ust-Ruditskaya factory near Oranienbaum outside St Petersburg. The great
Russian scholar had founded both the
factory and the workshop. In the course
of 4,000 chemical experiments he
worked out the composition and technology for producing smaltos —coloured
vitreous materials for use in mosaics,
thus reviving an art-form for which Early
Russian craftsmen had been famous,
but which had fallen into oblivion.
Of Lomonosov's twenty-one mosaics,
six are now in the Hermitage.

Russian eighteenth-century culture after Peter, in the "Age of Empresses", the
reigns of Anna Ioannovna, Elizabeth and Catherine II, is represented in two large
displays, located either side of the Dark Corridor — in Halls 162–167 (late 1720s
– early 1760s) and 168–174 (1760s to 1796, the reign of Catherine II).

The Display of Russian Culture of the Second Half of the 18th Century
(Hall 172)

The age of Catherine II is represented by a wide range of material from books and documents, furniture, porcelain and silver to a splendid collection of painted portraits by outstanding Russian and European artists.

Karl Christineck (1730/32– circa 1794)
Portrait of Count Alexei Bobrinsky as a Child. 1769. Oil on canvas
90 x 73.5 cm (Hall 170)

Unknown Artist of the Second Half of the 18th Century. *Portrait of Catherine II in a Travelling Dress*. Circa 1787
Oil on canvas. 52.2 x 65.8 cm

137

Nikolai Vereshchagin (1770 – circa 1814)
Vase. Circa 1798. Carved and engraved
walrus ivory. Height: 85 cm. (Hall 173)
In the rich collection of eighteenth-century
carved ivory — an old art form in which the
craftsmen of the Russian North excelled —
a special place is occupied by the exceptionally finely carved, elegant and harmonious
works of Nikolai Vereshchagin. He was not
a professional ivory carver, but worked for
a long time in the customs service at Arkhan-
gelsk and practised his beloved craft in his
leisure hours. This is one of a pair of vases
produced in the openwork carving technique and topped by a model of Falconet's
"Bronze Horseman". Beneath it and on the
body of the vase are medallions containing
portraits of Roman generals, monograms
and allegorical figures framed by garlands.
Vereshchagin presented his work to Catherine II and they were always kept in the palace collections.

Casket
Late 18th century. Made
by Rodion Leontyev, Tula
Blued, faceted and carved
steel, with gilded bronze
and velvet lining
18.5 x 27.5 x 19.2 cm
(Hall 173)
This is one of the masterpieces in the collection of
steel articles produced by
the celebrated craftsmen of
Tula. The strict Classical
forms of the casket are emphasized by bands of steel
beads and "cut-stones" —
the diamond-cut steel for
which Tula was especially
noted. More than 300 items
produced in the town south
of Moscow are now in the
Hermitage: guns, samovars,
toilet and writing sets, can-
dlesticks and even furniture.

Items from the Order of St George the Bringer of Victory Service
1777–78. Designed by Gavriil Kaslov, Gardner Factory, St Petersburg Porcelain, polychrome underglaze painting and gilding. (Hall 172)
The extremely rich collection of Russian porcelain includes formal tableware and sculpture from the eighteenth century produced not only at the Imperial Factory in St Petersburg, but also at the private factories that appeared in the 1760s. For example, Catherine II commissioned three Order Services from the factory of Francis Gardner, including the St George Service for eighty people. The decoration of the service features the badge and ribbon of the chivalric order. The service was intended for the receptions given each year for members of the order on the anniversary of its foundation.

Vladimir Borovikovsky (1757–1825)
Portrait of Grand Duchess Yelena Pavlovna.
Before 1799. Oil on canvas
72 x 58 cm (Hall 170)
The Classicism of Catherine's era was softened at the end of the eighteenth century by the subtlety of intimate moods brought by the Sentimentalism that became fashionable in art and literature. It also characterized the work of Borovikovsky, one of the most talented portraitists of the turn of the nineteenth century. The portrait of Yelena Pavlovna, the second of the six daughters of Paul I and Maria Fiodorovna, was painted shortly before her marriage to the Prince of Mecklenburg-Schwerin and her departure from Russia.

The Russian 19th-Century Interior display.
An Empire-style Drawing-Room. First third of the 19th century. (Hall 184)
The Karelian birch from which the furniture set for this room was made was a fashionable material in the Empire period. Its bright golden hue. exquisite texture and beautiful grain combine most attractively with the clear, simple forms of Neo-Classical furniture, giving it an especial elegance.
The Hermitage's rich collection of applied art has made possible an exhibition showing trends in the furnishing of the living rooms of Russian palaces and manor-houses throughout the nineteenth century. The exhibition occupies parts of the former imperial apartment (Halls 176–187). Each room contains a planned combination of furniture, tapestries, carpets, paintings on the wall and small household items of high artistic value giving a picture of one of the century's prevailing styles.

The Russian 19th-Century Interior display. A State Drawing-Room in a Palace 1805–06. (Hall 187)
This was once the first drawing-room in a suite belonging to a succession of Russian Empresses. The display here today reproduces an Empire-style state room in the Winter Palace early in Alexander I's reign. The 26-piece furniture set was made to designs by Luigi Rusca (1758–1822) at the St Petersburg Tapestry Factory. On the wall is one of four tapestries that went with the set, a depiction of the goddess Diana in a chariot.

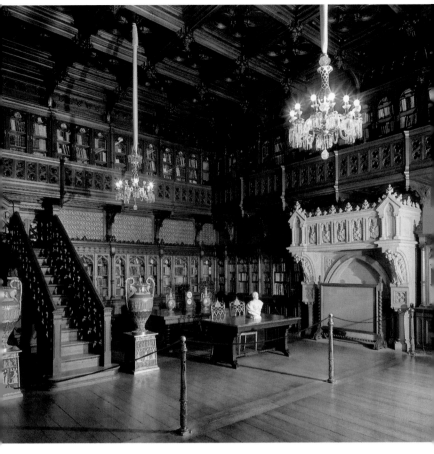

The Library of Nicholas II. 1894–96
Architect: Alexander Krasovsky. (Hall 178)
This is one of the few private rooms of
Nicholas II to have completely retained the
decoration and fittings designed by Alexander Krasovsky (1848–1923) who was in
charge of creating apartments for the young
Tsar in 1894–96. The architect removed
Briullov's existing decoration and finished
all the rooms very simply and unostentatiously. In the library, built-in furniture that
was then coming into fashion was used in
the palace for the first time. It was produced
to Krasovsky's designs at the Melzer and
Svirsky factory in St Petersburg. Carved walnut was used for the ceiling, the massive
tables, benches and bookcases that are set
against a background of gold-tooled red-leather panels. Seventeen bookcases below
line the walls completely, with more above.
Gothic motifs — linenfold pattern, trefoils
and quatrefoils — were used extensively
here, while the carved marble fireplace
seems part of a Gothic edifice. All this gave
the library an atmosphere of the past, and
of cosy quiet and concentration.

The Malachite Room. 1838–39
Architect: Alexander Briullov. (Hall 189)
Before the revolution this was the last state-room before the living apartments of the imperial couple and the starting-point for the formal processions that were an impor-tant part of palace ceremonial. In July 1917 the Winter Palace became the seat of the Provisional Government and the Malachite Room was used for meetings of the minis-ters until the government was overthrown on the night of 25 October 1917.

The Malachite Room was created by Briullov in place of the Jasper Room that perished in the fire of 1837. For its decoration 133 poods (over two tonnes) of malachite were used, taken from the enormous deposits found in the 1830s at one of the mines in the Urals belonging to the prominent mine-owning Demi-dov family. The combination of green malachite, white artificial-marble walls, abundant gilding on the doors and ceiling and crimson upholstery give the room a special festive elegance.

Malachite is a very rare coloured mineral. In the nineteenth century it was mined only in the Urals, usually in quite small pieces. A craftsman would cut these into thin slices, select them for their pattern and then use a special mastic to attach them to a prepared base before grinding and polishing the surface of the article. It was this technique, known as "Russian mosaic", that was used both for the ele-ments of decor in the Malachite Room and the malachite articles displayed there.

The Malachite Room
Malachite items
(Hall 189)
Showcases in the Malachite Room contain malachite table ornaments produced in Russia in the nineteenth century. They include, for example, a paperweight with a gilded porcelain figure of a woman in a laurel wreath symbolizing Russia holding a shield bearing the names of the fortresses captured in the Russo-Turkish War of 1828–29.

Cupboard with a mosaic panel "Tropical Forest"
1888–92. Peterhof Lapidary Works
Mahogany, gilded bronze and Florentine mosaic (chalcedony, sardonyx, jasper, malachite, opal, Koktebel pebbles, granite, lapis lazuli, petrified wood)
148 x 72 x 40 cm
(Hall 189)
This cupboard was commissioned by Alexander III and Empress Maria Fiodorovna for the Anichkov Palace, their preferred residence in St Petersburg.

The Small (White) Dining Room
1894–96. Architect: Alexander Krasovsky
(Hall 188)
This small room with windows overlooking
a small inner courtyard is where Nicholas
II's family took their meals. The decor is
stylized after the Rococo. Moulded frames
of rocaille scrolls, garlands and roses frame
areas of the walls and the tapestries made
in the St Petersburg factory. Three of the
tapestries belong to the *Parts of the World*
series, the fourth, above the fireplace, is
called *Swans*. On the mantelpiece is a clock
stopped at ten past two and a plaque commemorating the fact that at that time, in
the early hours of 26 October (7 November,
New Style) 1917 the Provisional Government was arrested in this room. The white
furniture, the cabinet containing eight-
eenth- and nineteenth-century glassware
and the eighteenth-century English crystal
chandelier with a musical mechanism recreate the authentic appearance of this historical interior.

The Rotunda
Early 1830s; 1838–39
Architects: Auguste Montferrand;
Alexander Briullov
(Hall 156)

A round hall at the intersection of the northern and western wings of the Winter Palace, connecting the private apartments to each other and to the more public part of the building, the Rotunda is covered by a glazed dome and encircled by a light metal gallery supported on brackets. Placed in the centre of the room is a reconstructed model of an unrealized monument to Russia's victories in the Northern War (1700–21) that Peter the Great proposed to set up in St Petersburg. The column itself is made of authentic bronze cylinders bearing relief depictions of the victories — masters from which a model was produced in Peter's turnery. It is crowned with a figure of the Tsar after the original by Rastrelli.

Unknown Artist. *Portrait of Empress Catherine I* (1684–1717). 1710s
Oil on canvas. (Hall 151)

Martha Skavronskaya, the daughter of a Lithuanian peasant was captured by the Russians when they took Marienburg (Aluksne in Latvia). In 1703 or 1704 she became the mistress of Peter the Great. She converted to Orthodoxy, taking the name Catherine, and became the Tsar's wife. Shortly before his death in 1725 she was crowned Empress and after Peter's death was herself proclaimed ruler, reigning until 1727.

This is one of the works in the recreated Romanov Gallery, the collection of portraits that hung in the Small Hermitage before the revolution. The recreation of the gallery was made possible by the wealth of the museum's stocks of portraits, works by both Russian and Western European artists who produced official images to commission for the Winter Palace and other residences.

145

Louis Tocqué (1696–1772)
Portrait of Empress Elizabeth (1709–1761)
1758. Oil on canvas
262 x 204 cm. (Hall 151)
Elizabeth, the daughter of Peter the Great and Catherine I, became empress in November 1741 as the result of a palace coup accomplished with the aid of the guards. During Elizabeth's reign Russia's international standing grew and autocracy strengthened, while Moscow University and the St Petersburg Academy of Arts were founded. Tocqué, one of the French King's finest portraitists, was invited to the Russian court where he painted this likeness of the Empress.

Unknown Artist
Portrait of Tsesarevich Piotr Fiodorovich (1728–1762), from 1761 Emperor Peter III
Late 1750s. Oil on canvas. (Hall 151)
Karl Peter Ulrich, the son of Karl Friedrich, Duke of Holstein (and nephew of King Charles XII of Sweden), and Anna, the daughter of Peter the Great, was invited to Russia by his childless aunt Elizabeth. After converting to Orthodoxy as Piotr Fiodorovich, he was declared her heir in 1742. In 1745 Piotr Fiodorovich was married to Princess Sophie Frederike Auguste of Anhalt-Zerbst, who became Grand Duchess Yekaterina (Catherine) Alexeyevna. Peter III managed to reign for just six months after his aunt's death in December 1761. His wife had him deposed in June 1762 and took the throne herself as Catherine II.

Yegor Botman (?–1891)
Paul I with Grand Dukes Alexander
Pavlovich and Konstantin Pavlovich and
the Hungarian Palatine Stephen Joseph
1840s. Oil on canvas. (Hall 151)
This work belongs to the "historical
portrait" type and reproduces an episode in the reign of Emperor Paul I
(1754–1801; Emperor from 1796).
The Emperor is depicted with his
two elder sons, his heir, the future
Alexander I, and Konstantin.

Unknown Artist
Portrait of Emperor Nicholas II
(1868–1918). 1915–16
Oil on canvas (Hall 153)
Nicholas II, son of Alexander III and
Empress Maria Fiodorovna, became
emperor in 1894. He was the last Russian
tsar and was shot with his family in 1918.

Unknown Artist. *Portrait of Emperor*
Alexander III (1845–1894). Late 19th century
Oil on canvas. (Hall 153)
Alexander III, the second son of Alexander II
and Empress Maria Alexandrovna, became
heir to the throne after the death of his elder
brother Nikolai. He came to the throne following his father's assassination in 1881.

The Concert Hall. 1791–93; 1830; 1837–39. Architects: Giacomo Quarenghi; Auguste Montferrand; Vasily Stasov (Hall 190)

The Concert Hall is the last in the Neva enfilade of state rooms. In 1922 the shrine of Alexander Nevsky, brought from the monastery that bears his name, was installed in this hall. It was created by craftsmen of the St Petersburg Mint in 1745–51 on the orders of Empress Elizabeth to contain the relics of the princely warrior saint. (Peter the Great had had them brought from Vladimir back in 1724.) About one and a half tonnes of silver was used to make the shrine. Behind the sarcophagus stands a pyramid framed by pedestals bearing military attributes. In the centre of it is an allegorical relief of Faith leading Alexander Nevsky. Depicted on he front wall of the sarcophagus are Alexander Nevsky's great victories: the battle against the Swedes on the Neva in 1240, the battle with the knights of the Livonian Order on frozen Lake Chud and the liberation of Pskov in 1242.

**The Concert Hall
Detail of the decoration**
The hall intended for palace concerts was decorated with sculptures of the nine muses.

The Great (Nicholas) Hall

1791–93; 1837–39
Architects: Giacomo
Quarenghi; Vasily Stasov
(Hall 191)
This, the central hall in the
Neva enfilade, is the largest
in the Winter Palace with a
floor area of 1,103 square
metres (almost 12,000
square feet). After 1856 it
was known as the Nicholas
Hall and contained a for-
mal portrait of Nicholas I.
Designed by Quarenghi and
restored by Stasov in strict
Classical style, this grand,
majestic hall served as the
setting for great court balls.
Today it is used for large
temporary exhibitions from
other museums.

Forehall

1791–93; 1837–39. Architects: Giacomo
Quarenghi; Vasily Stasov. (Hall 192)
This room, the first in the Neva enfilade
after leaving the Main Staircase, is decorated in the strict, grand, monumental
style of Classical architecture. A painting
entitled *The Sacrifice of Iphigenia* adorns
its ceiling. Standing in the centre of the
hall is the Malachite Rotunda originally
created in 1836 for St Isaac's Cathedral
on a commission from Anatoly Demidov.
Now the Forehall is used to house temporary exhibitions.

The Department of the East

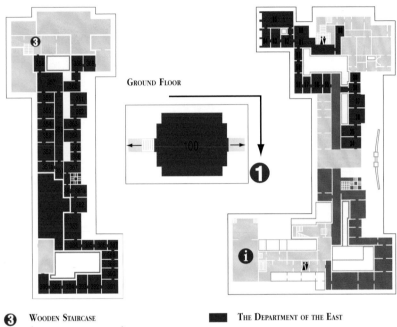

GROUND FLOOR

❸ WOODEN STAIRCASE
(ACCESS TO THE FIRST FLOOR)

❶ MAIN (JORDAN) STAIRCASE
(ACCESS TO THE FIRST FLOOR)

■ THE DEPARTMENT OF THE EAST

■ THE DEPARTMENT OF ARCHAEOLOGY

The Department of the East is among the younger departments in the Hermitage. It was created in 1920, although its stocks had already begun to accumulate in the reign of Catherine II. The collection of artefacts representing the culture and art of the countries of the East in the Hermitage is large and varied, as is the culture of the East itself. There can be no unity here — eastern culture reflects thousands of years of development of peoples and civilizations, some of which have disappeared, others have changed, while others still exist today. Naturally the formation of the Hermitage collection was shaped by the peculiarities, in terms of geography and time, of this huge region. The ancient period is reflected in the Ancient Egyptian, Mesopotamian, Assyrian and Palmyran collections, dating between the fourth millennium B.C. and the fourth century A.D. The mediaeval period, extending from the first millennium A.D. to the nineteenth century, is reflected by items from the Near and Middle East. The culture of Byzantium, which was connected with the East, is treated separately. India is represented by seventeenth- to twentieth-century exhibits. The Far Eastern collection includes items, chiefly from China, Japan and Indonesia, with a tremendous chronological span, from the third millennium B.C. to the twentieth century. A special place is occupied by items from the area of Central Asia, reflecting the culture and art of its peoples from the fourth millennium B.C. to the present day, and the peoples of the Caucasus from the tenth century B.C. to the nineteenth century.

The Hall of Ancient Egyptian Culture and Art (5th millennium B.C. to 1st millennium A.D.). (Hall 100)
The first Ancient Egyptian artefacts found their way to Russia in the eighteenth century, but the stocks were really formed in 1825 with the acquisition of the Castiglione collection.

Statue of Pharaoh Amenemhat III
Circa 1850–1800 B.C.
Granite. Height: 86.5 cm
(Hall 100)
This statue belongs to the canonical type of funerary sculpture intended for the tomb of a pharaoh. According to Ancient Egyptian conceptions, the statue was the receptacle for the soul of the deceased ruler and so its features were a portrait likeness of Amenemhat III.

151

Statue of the goddess Sekhmet-Mut
15th century B.C.
Granite. Height: 200 cm
(Hall 100)
Sokhmet, the daughter of Ra, the supreme god of Egypt, and the goddess of war and baking heat, was depicted as a woman with a lioness's head. In her hand the terrible deity holds an *ankh* — a symbol of life. The Hermitage statue was made, together with numerous similar ones, for the temple of the goddess at Karnak, the largest temple complex in Ancient Egypt.

Statuette of a man. Late 15th century B.C. Wood. Height: 34.5 cm (Hall 100)
This statuette was made by an unknown craftsman of the New Kingdom era, a period when Egyptian culture flourished. The male figure is presented in a traditional canonical pose — the trunk straight, the left leg advanced as if taking a step, the arms lowered. Yet for all this frozen conventionality, there is a certain plastic freedom and elegance of a kind about this piece. It is among the masterpieces of the Hermitage collection.

Stele of the royal scribe Ipi. Early 14th century B.C. Limestone. 95 x 71 cm (Hall 100)

This stele was found in the tomb of a scribe who occupied a fairly exalted position in Egyptian society. The deceased official is presented before Anubis, the god of the dead who was traditionally depicted in the form of a man with the head of a jackal. In his right hand Anubis holds the symbol of life, in his left a sceptre. In keeping with the usual rules of Ancient Egyptian art, the figures are depicted in profile, but with the shoulders facing the viewer.

Statue of Queen Arsinoe II. 4th century B.C. Basalt (Hall 100)

In 322 B.C. Egypt was conquered by the Greeks. Egyptian sculptors of the Hellenistic period strove to preserve the distinctive features of the national style and in this period produced idealized images true to the age-old tradition. This is true of the statue of Arsinoe II, although she holds a cornucopia or horn of plenty, something unknown in Egypt before the arrival of the Greeks. Some researchers contend that this statue is in fact a depiction of the legendary Queen Cleopatra of Egypt.

The Hall of Elephants
Display of murals
7th–8th centuries. Varakhsha, Sogdiana, Central Asia
Fresco. Height: 150–200 cm
These frescoes from a palace
that was buried in the sands
were uncovered by archaeologists in the 1960s at the site
of Varakhsha near Bukhara
in Uzbekistan. They are a
masterpiece of the art of
Sogdiana, a state that existed
in Central Asian until the
Arab conquest in the eighth
century. The main motif in
the frescoes is the ruler on
a slowly advancing elephant
and the predators attacking
him. Expressive line, an elevated rhythm and an elegant
combination of patches of
red and yellow are distinctive components of a style
that formed under the influence of ancient Indian art.

The Airtam Frieze (detail)
1st century. Central Asia. Carved limestone
This detail of a sculptural frieze depicting three musicians was found by chance in the waters of the River
Amu-Darya near Airtam in 1932. The subsequent archaeological investigation uncovered the walls of a Buddhist
temple from the first century A.D. and several more fragments of the frieze. They reflected the local way of life
(hairstyles and types of jewellery) as well as motifs from
Buddhist art (musicians, garlands of flowers) and Classical art (acanthus leaves).

Cultural and artistic monuments from Central Asia form the stocks of a special
section of the Department of the East and are displayed in ground floor halls of
the Winter Palace (№№33, 34–39) facing the Admiralty and Palace Square.* These
stocks span an immense period in the history of the peoples of the Central Asian
region from the fourth millennium B.C. to the nineteenth century.

The Caucasus and Central Asia

Figure of a winged deity
8th century B.C. Urartu, Caucasus. Bronze, ivory and stone with traces of gilding. Height: 16cm (Hall 56)
This figure of a winged lion with a human face served, it is suggested, as a throne ornament. It was found during excavations carried out in the mountains of Armenia in the later nineteenth century. It entered the Hermitage in 1885 and was then one of the few known examples of the art of Urartu, a state that existed between the ninth and sixth centuries B.C. and is known chiefly from mentions in ancient Assyrian texts.

Bowls. 9th–6th century B.C. Urartu, Caucasus
Bronze. Diameter: 20 cm (Hall 56)
Ninety-seven bronze bowls of faultlessly regular shape (eleven of which are now in the Hermitage) were found in a secret hiding-place at the Urartian fortress of Teishebaini that Boris Piotrovsky's expedition excavated on Karmir-Blur hill. It is believed that the bowls were hidden at a moment of danger when the fortress was being besieged by Scythians. The names of rulers of Urartu are engraved on the bottoms of the bowls. The beauty of their clear, simple shapes is brought out by skilful polishing that has given an enduring shine to the metal. The bowls possess a special quality: when tapped they produce a melodic ring and each has its own tone.

A study of the culture of Urartu was made in the course of many years of excavations in the 1930s and 1940s on the Karmir-Blur hill in upland Armenia. The work was led by Boris Piotrovsky (1908–1990), a prominent scholar who later became director of the Hermitage. The Urartian works he discovered are included in the display of the culture and art of the Caucasus located in the ground-floor halls of the Winter Palace that face the courtyard (Halls 55–61). The exhibits present the history and culture of the peoples of the Caucasus over more than a thousand years, from the tenth or ninth century B.C. to the fifteenth century A.D.

155

**St Gregory the Wonderworker
(Thaumaturgus).** 12th century. Byzantium
Tempera on gessoed panel. 81 x 53 cm
(Hall 382)
This image of Gregory, a third-century
bishop of Neo-Caesarea (Pontus), who
converted many pagans and became a
much-venerated saint, is one of the mas-
terpieces in the Hermitage's collection of
Byzantine icons.

The art of Byzantium — a mediaeval
state in the Eastern Mediterranean that
endured for almost a thousand years,
from the fourth century to the fourteenth, and became a bulwark of Chris-
tendom — is represented in the Hermitage by stocks that are small in
number, but superb in quality. They
include a world-famous collection of
silver vessels, outstanding pieces of
carved ivory, lead seals and a valuable
group of icons.

Diptych with a depiction of circus scenes
5th century. Byzantium. Ivory. 33 x 10.5 cm
(Hall 381a)
This superb diptych was a sort of notebook
for a nobleman, a consul who, as was customary, organized a circus performance
to mark his election. This early work, still
transfused with the spirit of Antiquity, already displays the ornamental abstraction
that would mark Christian art.

Paten of Bishop Paternus. 491–518
Byzantium. Gilded silver with paste and
stones. Diameter: 61 cm (Hall 381a)
This plate for the Eucharistic bread was, the
Latin inscription tells us, "renewed from an
old one" for the Bishop of the city of Tomis
(present-day Constanta in Romania). It was
among other items in a famous hoard found
in 1912 in the village of Maloye Pereshchepi-
no, near Poltava in the Ukraine.

Bronze aquamanile in the shape of a zebu cow
1206. Ali ibn Muhammad ibn Abu-l-Qasim, Iran
Cast bronze inlaid with silver. Height: 35 cm (Hall 384)
This aquamanile (water jug) depicting a zebu cow feeding her calf while being attacked by a leopard was created with exceptional skill and expressiveness by a mediaeval craftsman who recorded his name in an Arabic inscription. The museum can boast one of the world's largest collections of Iranian artefacts.

Kettle. 1163. Herat, Iran
Cast and raised bronze (brass) with silver and copper inlay. Height: 18.5 cm (Hall 384)

Dish bearing a depiction of Shapur II out hunting
4th century. Sassanid Iran
Chased silver. Diameter: 22.9 cm (Hall 383)
Iran under the Sassanid dynasty was famous for its art and especially artistic metal-working. The Hermitage's collection of Sassanid silver is one of the best outside of Iran itself and is known all over the world. One of the masterpieces of the collection is a dish bearing a hunting scene — the King drawing his bow while still in the saddle of his racing steed and a fierce lion that is depicted twice, fighting for its life and defeated — skilfully inscribed in a circle. The expressive, monumental composition with its finely worked details make this silver bowl a truly "royal" piece of work.

Wine jug bearing a depiction of a Senmurv. 5th–6th centuries. Sassanid Iran. Silver with gilding (Hall 383)
This finely proportioned jug with a tall handle of a typical Iranian shape is decorated with a chased image of a mythical being called a Senmurv — a dog-bird that was considered a symbol of fertility.

Vase bearing a depiction of a game of polo. 13th century. Iran. Earthenware with lustre glaze. Height: 80 cm (Hall 387)
This is a rare and outstanding example of Iranian mediaeval pottery. Its surface is divided into five tiers containing relief depictions of plants, birds and exquisite animals.

Lamp. 1346–47. Syria or Egypt
Glass and enamel. Height: 36.2 cm
(Hall 390)
This elaborately shaped lamp embellished with heraldic devices and Arabic inscriptions that mention the name of the sultan for whom it was made is one of the typical examples of mediaeval Islamic art from the Middle Eastern glass collection.

Mihr-Ali. *Portrait of Fath Ali Shah.* Iran. 1809–10 Oil on canvas. 253 x 124 cm (Hall 393)

This formal portrait of Fath Ali Shah, a ruler of Iran from the Qajar dynasty that was in power from 1796 to 1925, is evidence of the intrusion of European traditions into Islamic art. The ban on the depiction of human beings has been disregarded and easel-painting techniques employed. Yet at the same time the image obeys certain rules: a rigid pose and sharp outline, the ornamental quality of the refinedly elegant details that conceals the still unaccustomed three-dimensionality of the figure. All of this serves to create an "unearthly" image of the ruler like the kings of old.

The art of the Middle East — Byzantium, Iran, Iraq, Syria, Turkey and mediaeval Egypt — forms one of the large sections of the Department of the East. Its displays are located on the second floor of the Winter Palace (Halls 381–397), in rooms overlooking the Admiralty and the Neva that were once the apartments of Nicholas I and his grandson Alexander III (1881–1894).

The display of Far Eastern art occupies Halls 351–366 on the second floor of the Winter Palace.

**The Pure Land
of the Amida Buddha**
Khara-Khoto, Tibet
Natural paints on canvas.
99 x 63.8 cm
This remarkable example of a Tibetan religious image was discovered by Piotr Kozlov's expedition in the ancient city of Khara-Khoto that stood on the edge of the Gobi Desert. The city was a major centre in the state of Hsi Hsia formed by the Tangut people of Central Asia in the tenth century. It perished in the thirteenth century and was buried by the sands. By isolating them from the air, the sand splendidly preserved priceless wood engravings and paintings on paper, silk and canvas. The Buddha is depicted standing on two lotuses. Two Bodhisattvas hold a lotus flower that is a symbol of purity in the Buddhist religion offering it for the soul of the saint to walk upon, as on: "pure land, unsullied by sin". The saint himself is depicted in the lower left-hand corner of the elaborate composition. The space around the figures is filled with depictions of musical instruments that play themselves.

Head of a Bohisattva
8th century. Tun-huang (Dunhuang), China
Clay, natural paints.
Height: 37 cm
An expedition led by the St Petersburg academician Sergei Oldenburg discovered one of the leading centres of mediaeval China, the Cave of the Thousand Buddhas monastery (Ch'ien-fo Tung) near to Tun-huang, a city at the start of the Great Silk Road. The walls of the caves still retained remarkable examples of murals, as well as monumental sculpture created from soft, porous loess clay. The Bodhisattvas, enlightened beings second in significance after the Buddhas, are supposed to help to save all living things on Earth. The seventh- to ninth-century time of the Tang dynasty saw Chinese culture flourish with the appearance of porcelain, the use of paper and book-printing. Buddhism reached China from India by way of Central Asia in the first century A.D. and it had a major influence on the shaping of Chinese art.

The Buddha of Healing
Khara-Khoto, Tibet
Natural paints on canvas.
(Hall 364)
The Buddha of Healing
is depicted sitting in the
traditional lotus position,
dressed in red clothing
that is stylized to resemble
a monk's robe sewn from
rags. In his hand he holds
his invariable attribute,
a bowl of the medicinal
myrobalan fruit. Depicted
alongside the Buddha are
two Bodhisattvas, a white
one with a symbol of the
moon and a flesh-coloured
one with a symbol of the
sun. In all the composition
contains thirty-nine per-
sonages, including seven
accompanying Buddhas
whose figures are placed in
the upper part of the icon,
as well as a variety of deities belonging to both the
Hindu and Buddhist realms.

Guhyamantrayana. 18th century. Tibet
Gilded bronze. Height: 24 cm
This deity belongs to the pantheon of
Tantric Buddhism or Mantrayana. This
form of Buddhism is better known as
Vajrayana, the Vehicle of the Diamond
(or Thunderbolt), and is a "mystic" form
of the religion that appeared in the early
centuries A.D. in the Buddhist monaster-
ies of northern India. In the seventh and
eighth centuries the Vajrayana reached
Tibet where it merged with local cults and
developed into what we now know as
Tibetan Buddhism. The word Guhyamantrayana means "hidden vehicle of the
mantra". The deity Guhyamantrayana
belongs to the class of personal guardian
or tutelary deities.

Unknown artist
Portrait of an Official
11th–12th century. Khara-Khoto, China. India ink on paper. 45 x 31.8 cm
A first-class example of the portraiture of the Sung era, part of the period when this genre flourished in China, and a very rare example of graphic art found together with painted scrolls, sculpture and a large number of books in the "ghost-city" of Khara-Khoto. The face of the elderly official is carefully drawn, something characteristic of Chinese portraiture and connected with the concepts of Chinese physiognomy which postulated a magical link between the shape of the face and a person's destiny.

Dish with peonies. Late 17th – early 18th century. China Porcelain with *famille jaune* painting. Diameter: 34.5 cm
The Chinese themselves date the appearance of porcelain to the end of the first millennium B.C. The Hermitage stocks include a very rich collection of superb Chinese porcelain. Richness of colour is a characteristic of pieces with overglaze painting produced in the seventeenth and eighteenth centuries. Painting on the glaze required a lower firing temperature in order to preserve its colourfulness.

Basin for fish. First quarter of the 18th century. China. Porcelain with *famille jaune* painting. Diameter: 36.3 cm
The heyday of porcelain production in China came at the turn of the eighteenth century when they began to decorate articles with painting in five or six colours dominate either by a strong green (*famille jaune*) or a rose-pink (*famille rose*). Elegant, finely-worked painting in which flowers and birds were the chief elements, brings out the beautiful perfection of the shapes for vessels that established themselves in China over many centuries.

162

The Far East

Bowl on an annular base
Second half of the 16th century. China
Porcelain with cobalt painting.
Height: 16 cm; diameter: 32.5 cm
Cobalt paint was often used to decorate
porcelain articles as it could withstand
a high kiln temperature. It was applied
to the surface of the piece before it was
covered with glaze and fired.

Netsuke *Hetai with a Fan*
Late 18th – early 19th century. Kyoto or
Osaka school, Japan. Ivory. Height: 4 cm
The traditional Japanese kimono has
no pockets. As a result, in the seventeenth century netsuke appeared as
decorative toggles at one end of a silk
cord that could be tucked behind the
obi (sash belt). The other end of the
cord might be attached to a tobacco
pouch, a bunch of keys, or an *inro*,
a lacquer box with several compartments. Netsuke became one of the
main adornments of Japanese dress.

**Figure of a Lion of Fo with a pearl
in its paws.** Late 17th – early 18th century. China. Earthenware with enamelling
and painting

Hasetalawa Ikko
Netsuke *A Boy Drawing Ame-No Uzume*
Late 18th – early 19th century. Japan
Ivory. Height: 4 cm
The subjects of netsuke are very varied,
embracing history, literature, mythology,
popular beliefs, good luck symbols and
the everyday life of the Japanese.

The Department of Archaeology

GROUND FLOOR

The displays of the Department of Archaeology are located in rooms on the ground floor of the north-western part of the Winter Palace (Halls 11–26), including what is known as the Kutuzov Corridor (Halls 24 and 33). The rooms with windows overlooking the Admiralty and the Neva were in the past part of the Large Imperial Apartments. One of them (Hall 17) was once the study of Emperor Nicholas I and contained the camp-bed on which he died in 1854. The rooms adjoining the study (Halls 11–16) were intended for the Tsar's children. Some of these have retained their historical appearance. In the Gothic Drawing-Room, for example, once the state drawing-room of Grand Duchess Olga Nikolayevna, we can still see elements of Neo-Gothic decor. In Hall 13 the Rococo-style finish has partially survived. It was created by Stakenschneider for the wedding of Nicholas I's youngest son, Grand Duke Nikolai (Nicholas) Nikolayevich.

▨ THE DEPARTMENT OF ARCHAEOLOGY
▨ THE DEPARTMENT OF THE EAST

The stocks of the Department of Archaeology number some 400,000 items. It is one of the most significant archaeological collections in the country and the world, containing artefacts of primitive cultures that existed on territory that became the Russian Empire over a period between the Early Stone Age, 400,000 years ago, to late Antiquity (the second and third centuries A.D.) and the early Middle Ages (seventh to eleventh centuries). The formation of these stocks began back in the eighteenth century with what is known as the Siberian Collection of Peter the Great* — golden ornaments that were removed from ancient Siberian burial mounds by treasure-hunters and presented to Tsar Peter by the early industrialist and Urals mining magnate Akinfy Demidov. Systematic archaeological explorations began in 1837 in the south of Russia, in the area of the Black Sea. It is from there that the Hermitage's collection of Scythian and Sarmatian items come. In 1859 the Imperial Archaeological Commission was established. It directed fieldwork across the country and passed the most outstanding finds to the Hermitage. These were supplemented by items from hoards discovered by chance. After the revolution private collections came into the museum. The main source of "new" antiquities today are the expeditions organized by the Department of Archaeology that was established in 1931.

The Department of Archaeology

**The display of the Department of Archaeology
The Gothic Drawing-Room**
1838–39. Architect:
Alexander Briullov (Hall 12)
On display here are very
ancient items from the
Stone Age: Lower Palaeo-
lithic tools from Satani-
Dar hill in Armenia; pre-
historic works of art from
Malta, an early human
camping place discovered
near Irkutsk, and stones
brought from Lake Onega
(Karelia) that bear 4000-
year-old Neolithic petro-
glyphs.

**The display of the Department
of Archaeology. The hall with cupids**
1856. Architect: Andrei Stakenschneider
(Hall 13)
This hall and its neighbours contain unique
archaeological complexes: material from
a Neolithic settlement discovered during
peat-cutting operations at the Shigirsky
moor in Yekaterinburg region (the Urals);
finds from settlements of the Tripolye culture of the first farmers — a pottery vessel
and statuettes of female deities; Bronze-
Age artefacts from the Caucasus — from
the famous Maikop burial mound (mid-
third-millennium B.C.) and from the
Koban culture (ninth to eighth centuries
B.C.), found during excavations by the
settlement of that name in 1868.

Bear-Man. 1st–3rd century. Ilyinskoye
village, Perm region, Urals
Bronze. Height: 8 cm
This little figure on bear's legs is a striking
example of the "Animal Style" typical of
primitive art from the forest zone of
Eurasia. The beast that resembles a human
being, able to stand on two legs, strong
and intelligent is a totem image, a guardian of the clan or tribe, venerated
as its ancestor.

Idol. Second half of the 2nd millennium B.C. Galich district, Kostroma Region, Russia
Copper. Height: 14 cm (Hall 14)
This is a depiction of a deity or ancestral spirit in accordance with the beliefs of the people who inhabited Russia's forest zone in the early Bronze Age. It comes from the Galich Hoard, discovered in 1836 on the shore of Lake Galich in north-east European Russia. The idol, a very ancient example of artistic casting work, has a mysterious eloquence and an imposing decorativeness.

Head of a doe-elk
2nd millennium B.C. Urals
Horn. Length: 19.5 cm (Hall 13)
This is one of the masterpieces of art created at the dawn of human history, in the Neolithic Period or New Stone Age. This sculptural head of a female elk has been carved from horn with striking accuracy and a knowledge of the specific features of the animal, yet without unnecessary fine detail, betraying a subtle grasp of form. The symbolic, emblematic nature of the image is organically combined with decorativeness. This sculpture may have served as the handle of a ritual vessel or the tip of a staff. It entered the Hermitage in 1914 together with other finds from the Shigirsky peat deposits. The peat preserved all the artefacts that were found it: tools and works of art made from horn, wood and stone shedding light on the life and labours of forest-dwelling hunter-fishermen who lived in the Urals over four thousand years ago.

Griffin with a deer's head in its beak

5th–4th century B.C.
2nd Pazyryk burial mound, Pazyryk, Altai mountains, Southern Siberia. Wood and leather. Height: 27 cm (Hall 22)

The fantastic bird-like griffin and the deer that would have been familiar to any ancient Altai hunter are here combined in a vivid image of formidable strength and beauty. This magnificent example of the art of the ancient nomads of southern Siberia was found during excavation of one of the burial mounds at the Pazyryk site in the Altai mountains. This was the burial ground for tribal leaders who were interred in deep pits together with a host of precious objects thought to be needed in the afterlife. The pits were then covered with heaps of stones. Water penetrating down through the stones froze, forming permafrost that preserved items made of perishable materials such as wood, leather, felt and fabrics. Thanks to archaeological investigations of the Pazyryk burials carried out (with intervals) between 1929 and 1949, the Hermitage came into possession of a collection of ancient artefacts that are unique in their richness, state of preservation and artistic value (Halls 22, 23, 25 and 26).

Vessel bearing a depiction of an animal against a mountain background.

Mid-3rd millennium B.C. Maikop, Northern Caucasus. Silver
Height: 9.6 cm (Hall 14)

It is possible to recognize the shape of the Caucasus range in the jagged lines on this vessel that comes from the Maikop burial mound, excavated in 1897 by the noted Russian

archaeologist Nikolai Veselovsky. The artificial mound was found to contain the burial of a chieftain and members of his tribe surrounded by a large number of precious objects — gold and silver figures of bullocks, plaques, diadems, necklaces, beads and vessels. This is one of the richest archaeological complexes discovered on Russian territory.

167

Pile carpet. Detail
5th–4th century B.C.
5th Pazyryk burial mound,
Pazyryk, Altai mountains,
Southern Siberia. Wool
200 x 185 cm (Hall 25)
This is the oldest pile carpet in the world. It is almost a thousand years old-
er than the earliest known
carpet from Iran, where
carpet-weaving began in
the fourteenth century.
Yet it is produced by one
of the same methods of
knotting that is still used
to make carpets today.
The density of the work
(3600 knots to each 10
centimetres), the exquisite
colours and design — ornamental strips and a procession of animals in several
sections) make the carpet
a true masterpiece.

Chariot. 5th–4th century B.C. 5th Pazyryk burial mound,
Pazyryk, Altai mountains, Southern Siberia. Wood
and leather. Height: 300 cm (Hall 25)
This vehicle served as a hearse, used to convey the body
of the chieftain to the burial site. It was made of wooden
poles fastened with leather without a single nail.

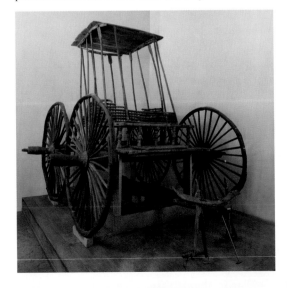

Carpet. 5th–4th century B.C. 5th Pazyryk burial mound, Pazyryk, Altai mountains, Southern Siberia Coloured felt, appliqué 4.5 x 6.5 metres (Hall 26) This huge carpet served as the covering of a burial tent. Sewn onto it in two rows are monumental coloured felt figures, about two metres high.

Swan. 5th–4th century B.C. 5th Pazyryk burial mound, Pazyryk, Altai mountains, Southern Siberia. Felt Length: 29 cm (Hall 26) The burial contained several felt figures of swans. In the ancient perception of the world, the swan was regarded as an embodiment of three natural elements — water, air and earth.

The display of the Department of Archaeology
5th–4th century B.C. 5th Pazyryk burial mound, Pazyryk, Altai mountains, Southern Siberia (Hall 26) The harness ornaments of wood and leather found in the Pazyryk burial mounds — works of art by the nomads of the Altai — are evidence of the high level of development reached in the crafts in the area of southern Siberia. Practical artefacts and works of art of local and distant origin — leather and fur clothing and footwear, earthenware jugs, Chinese silks — found in the tumuli of the Altai create an exceptionally full and vivid picture of the ancient culture of nomadic peoples.

The Gold Room

The display of the Gold Room is located in halls on the ground floor of the Winter Palace and made up of three sections. The first part contains gold artefacts found during archaeological excavations of ancient burial mounds over an area extending from the northern Black Sea coast and the Caucasus to eastern Siberia. The main interest here lies in the unique Siberian collection of Peter the Great, as well as the treasures from Scythian burials of the seventh and sixth centuries B.C. The next section of the display consists of remarkable pieces of Greek jewellery and gold artefacts discovered by archaeologists in the cemeteries of ancient settlements in the Crimea and adjacent areas. The work of jewellers from the East is on display in the last section of the Golden Treasury. Here visitors can admire the strikingly rich and opulently designed creations of craftsmen who worked in India, China, Turkey, Byzantium and Central Asia. Many of them were diplomatic gifts to the rulers of Russia.

The treasury was reopened after restoration in 1998. Special security measures mean that visitors can only view the display as part of an organized guided tour. The Jewellery Gallery— a collection of jewellery, articles made of gold and precious stones, diplomatic gifts, archaeological antiquities, cameos and intaglios — was founded by Catherine II. Today's Gold Room has its origins in that unique late-eighteenth-century collection.

Torque. 4th–3rd century B.C. Siberian collection of Peter the Great. Gold, turquoise and coral. Diameter: 13 cm
Between the seventh century B.C. and the first century A.D. south-western Siberia was home to the nomadic Sak tribes, relatives of the Scythians. Gold jewellery in what is known as the Animal Style that was found by grave robbers in Sak burials found its way into the Russian Tsar's Siberian collection at the start of the eighteenth century.

Plaque in the form of a panther coiled in a circle 7th–6th century B.C. Siberian collection of Peter the Great. Gold. Diameter: circa 11 cm
The Siberian collection consists mainly of openwork belt buckles, clasps, torques, earrings, rings, bracelets and plates that decorated horse harnesses. This solid cast plaque in the form of a panther is among the oldest items in this precious collection.

Deer. 7th–6th century B.C. Burial mound by the settlement Kostromskaya. Gold Length: 31.7 cm
This gold shield ornament in the form of a deer is a masterpiece of the Scythian Animal Style. It is striking for the perfect execution and the expressive pose. The craftsman has depicted the deer in flight, its neck stretched forward, its legs folded up to its belly. Specialists belief that the image of the deer had a magical significance and was associated with the sun and eternal life.

Comb. 4th century B.C. Solokha burial mound Gold. Height: 12.3 cm; width: 10.2 cm

This comb, apparently created by a Greek craftsman commissioned by a Scythian leader, is reminiscent of the classical facade of a Greek temple. The long, four-sided teeth play the role of columns; resting on them is the frieze made up of figures of lions. This in turn supports the pediment consisting of battling Scythian warriors. The figures of the warriors, horses and lions were soldered together from two halves, a pair of embossed plates, and were executed with the astonishing skill typical of Greek jewellery work.

Gorytos (case for a bow and arrows). 4th century B.C. Chertomlyk burial mound. Gold. Height: 68 cm; width: 27.3 cm

The 19-metre-high Chertomlyk burial mound by Nikopol (north of the Crimea) is among the very rich Scythian tombs referred to as "royal". In it archaeologists discovered gold and silver items of exceptional beauty and superb artistry produced by Greek craftsmen to commission from a Scythian. The gold covering of the quiver bears a scene from the life of the Ancient Greek hero Achilles.

172

Vessel bearing depictions of Scythians. 4th century B.C. Kul-Oba burial mound, Kerch
Electrum (an alloy of gold and silver). Height: 13 cm
This superb example of Greek work shows long-haired Scythians in typical clothing consisting of broad trousers (not customary for the Greeks), long jackets and peaked hats. It is hard to establish the exact subject.

Earring. 4th century B.C. Feodosian burial mound (made in Greece). Chased, cast and engraved gold with the use of "microtechnique". Height: 9 cm
The earrings found during the excavation of the grave of a rich Greek woman near Feodosia (Crimea) are a masterpiece of Greek jewellery work. They were made using an exceptionally complicated technique: attached to the disc is a semicircular piece, or crescent, decorated by a quadriga (a chariot drawn by four horses) driven by the god Apollo. The crescent itself is made of tiny elements soldered together, each of which is in turn a diamond or rhombus made up of four minute grains of gold.

Torque with Scythian horsemen
400–350 B.C. Kul-Oba burial mound, Kerch, Northern Black Sea coast
Gold and enamel. 26.6 x 24 cm
The torque, a kind of necklace, was a Scythian symbol of wealth and power. Attached to the ends are two figures of Scythian horsemen. The quality of the piece is testimony to the great mastery of the Greek jeweller who created it.

Diadem. 1st century A.D. Northern Black Sea area Novocherkassky hoard, Novorossiisk. Khokheag burial mound. Gold, turquoise, coral, garnet, amethyst, glass and pearl Circumference: 61 cm; height: 15 cm
In the third century B.C. the Scythians began to be driven from their lands by other nomads, the Sarmatians. Sarmatian burials have produced numerous items made of silver and precious stones that display less refined workmanship than Scythian articles. This diadem was probably created by a local Sarmatian craftsman. The centre of the piece is adorned by an exquisite Greek head carved from an amethyst. The diadem is crowned by a frieze of trees and animals that were evidently a symbol of life and the sun.

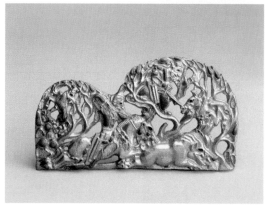

Belt buckle bearing a hunting scene
4th century B.C. Siberian collection of Peter the Great. Gold, turquoise, coral and glass Lenght: 19.7 cm
This belt buckle is embellished with a striking, dynamic scene of a warrior hunting a lion that would appear to have had magical power. The scene is skilfully worked into the ornament formed from tree branches among which there are the barely distinguishable figures of another man and a dog. The gold items from the Siberian collection are usually decorated with precious and semiprecious stones.

Burial mask of a king. 2nd century A.D.(?) Kerch
Gold. 22.5 x 15 cm
This mask was found in the necropolis of Panticapeum
(present-day Kerch), the capital of the kingdom known
as Cimmerian Bosporus that was founded on the northern
Black Sea coast by Greeks in the fifth century B.C.
The preparation of burial masks from the faces of the dead
was customary for Ancient Rome, under whose power the
Bosporan kingdom came. This gold mask does not seem to
have been made "mechanically" using a cast, and is more
likely a portrait full of a sense of dignified mourning.

Dagger and sheath
Late 16th – early 17th century. Turkey
Steel, jade, rubies, emeralds, spinel
Length: 27.3 cm

Jug. Body: 10th–11th century, Egypt; decoration: 17th century, Turkey
Carved rock crystal with gold and precious stones. Height: 16.8 cm
The surface of the crystal vessel is covered with carving in the form of geometric and plant ornament. The gold elements adorning the handles, neck and base of the jug were made considerably later, by Turkish craftsmen. The pieces made from rock crystal by mediaeval Egyptian craftsmen were highly prized both in Western Europe and in the Middle East where they were complemented by luxurious and costly mountings.

Table. 17th century. Situram (craftsman). India
Gold with diamonds, rubies, emeralds, pearls and enamel. 27.3 x 27.3 cm
This table was among a group of seventeen precious articles presented in 1741 by Nadir Shah, ruler of Iran, to the Russian Emperor Ivan VI (nine items), his mother, the regent Anna Leopoldovna (four) and Elizabeth, daughter of Peter the Great, (also four). The pieces came from the treasury of the Great Moguls, the rulers of India, that Nadir plundered when he invaded the subcontinent in 1738–39. In the autumn of 1739 he decided to send an embassy to Russia and Turkey, apparently to spread word of his victory. The embassy made very slow progress from India to Russia, quite probably because the gifts included fourteen live elephants. The back of the table bears the signature of the craftsman, an extremely rare instance of the name of an Indian jeweller appearing on his work.

Aigrette. India. 17th century
Jade, gold, diamonds, rubies, emeralds,
garnets and rock crystal. Height: 17.1 cm
This turban ornament that is a sign of the
owner's exalted pedigree was also among
the gifts from Nadir Shah. Its reverse is
also covered with small rubies and plant
ornament. There too is a special channel
to hold a plume. The aigrette was among
the items presented to Ivan VI.

Jug. India. 17th century. Gold, diamonds,
rubies and emeralds. Height: 26 cm
Jugs like this were apparently intended for
aromatic rose water. The large emeralds
on the body of the vessel are embellished
by engraving. This precious item from the
treasury of the Great Moguls was a gift to
Emperor Ivan VI.

Plate. India. 17th century
Gold, diamonds, rubies, emeralds
and enamel. Diameter: 19.7 cm
This plate apparently served as a base for
some sort of jug. In the centre of the reverse it bears a large carved rosette, from
which radiate ornamented appliqué strips.
The front side of the plate is divided into
eight segments completely covered by hun-
dreds of rubies of different shades, among
which enormous diamonds and emeralds
are scattered. This priceless gift was presented by the embassy to Ivan VI in the
name of Nadir Shah.

THE SMALL
HERMITAGE

The Pavilion Hall and Hanging Garden
Mediaeval Applied Art
The Low Countries,
15th–16th Centuries

FIRST FLOOR

The Small Hermitage is the smallest building in the Hermitage complex. It consists of the Hanging Garden, two pavilions at its north and south ends and two galleries that join them, flanking the garden on east and west.

THE LOW COUNTRIES, 15TH–16TH CENTURIES
MEDIAEVAL APPLIED ART
THE PAVILION HALL

The elements of the Small Hermitage were created at various times in the period from 1764 to 1775. All the work was supervised by the architect Yury Velten. First to be built, in 1764–66, was the Southern Pavilion, directly connected with Catherine II's apartments in the south-east part of the Winter Palace. It was known as "the Nearby House" or "the favourites' block" at that time. Later it was used as spare accommodation for the residence, and nowadays it houses the State Hermitage's library. At the same time as the Southern Pavilion, the Hanging Garden was created. Then, in 1767–69, at its opposite end the Northern Pavilion was erected. This pavilion contained six rooms: a large state room overlooking the Neva, connected by three open arches with the Orangery that gave onto the Hanging Garden, and four corner "cabinets". Here, surrounded by the paintings and curiosities of her museum, the Empress held her "hermitages", gatherings for the select few. In 1768–75 the galleries were built to house the growing collection that could no longer fit in the pavilion. In 1840–44 the galleries and the Hanging Garden were reconstructed by Vasily Stasov, while in 1850–58 his colleague Andrei Stakenschneider replaced Catherine's rooms in the Northern Pavilion with the single Pavilion Hall.

The Small Hermitage contains displays of Western European mediaeval applied art (Hall 259) and the art of the Low Countries from the fifteenth and sixteen centuries (Halls 258, 261, 262). The collection of mediaeval art, quite small in quantity, but of excellent quality, includes fine examples of all the main types of craft work: ivory carving, Limoges enamels, bronze aquamaniles, furniture, tapestries, silverware, pottery and more. The collection of Netherlandish art is not large either, but gives a thorough picture of the discoveries made by the region's painters and can boast individual masterpieces by Robert Campin, Rogier van der Weyden, Hugo van der Goes and Lucas van Leyden.

180

The Small Hermitage
The Northern Pavilion. 1767–69. Architect: Jean-Baptiste Vallin de la Mothe
This part of the Small Hermitage was long known as the La Mothe Pavilion after the French architect who created it. The relatively small building manages nevertheless to be exquisitely monumental. It adjoins the eastern facade of the Winter Palace, to which it is connected by a covered passageway. It matches the palace in height and division into storeys. In contrast, however, to its opulent "Baroque" neighbour, the facade of the Northern Pavilion of the Small Hermitage reflects the Classical style with its majestic restraint. The lowest part, in rusticated stone, serves as a base for an elegant

Corinthian colonnade that spans the two upper storeys. Above the cornice there is a sculptural group, while the colonnade is flanked by statues of the goddesses of flowers and fruit, Flora and Pomona, a reminder that in the eighteenth century the Northern Pavilion was also called "the Orangery House".
This garden of "the Russian Semiramis", as Catherine II was sometimes called, was constructed on the vaults of the lower storey of the Small Hermitage by Yury Velten (following Vallin de la Mothe's concept). In the 1840s Stasov created new masonry supports for the garden and installed waterproofing and a ventilation system. The garden is adorned by eighteenth-century sculpture and a fountain.

The Hanging Garden
1764–69; 1840–44
Architects: Yury Velten;
Vasily Stasov

The *Peacock* Clock
Second half of the 18th century. James Coxe, England
Wood, gilded bronze,
silver foit (Hall 204)
This clock with mechanical figures was the work of the celebrated clockmaker James Coxe. It was bought disassembled by Prince Grigory Potemkin and after his death passed to Catherine II. In 1792 it was assembled and put in working order by the mechanic Ivan Kulibin. On the hour, to the accompaniment of music and the chiming of bells, the peacock turns and spreads its tail, the cockerel crows and the owl blinks its eyes. The dial of the clock is in the cap of a mushroom.

Mosaic in the Pavilion Hall
Copy of the floor of a bath at Ocriculum, Rome
1847–51. Craftsmen from the St Petersburg
Academy of Arts. (Hall 204)

The Pavilion Hall
1850–58. Architect: Andrei
Stakenschneider. (Hall 204)
Erudition, fantasy and refined taste
are the hallmarks of the architect
Stakenschneider who created this
hall in place of the eighteenth-
century rooms. The combination of
Classical and Eastern motifs give the
hall a romantic air: open two-tier
arcades of white marble in the style
of the Italian Renaissance, lace-fine
Classical moulded ornament on the
arches and walls, and a Moorish
pattern in the balcony railings. Set
into the floor between the walls
bearing fountains that were made in
imitation of the famous "Fountain
of Tears" in the palace of the Crimean Khan at Bakhchiserai is a copy
of an Ancient Roman mosaic found
in 1780 during excavations of the
town of Ocriculum near Rome.

The Western Gallery. Display of mediaeval Western European applied art. (Hall 259)

The Fortuni Vase. Mid-14th century Malaga, Spain. Faience with lustre painting. Height: 11 cm. (Hall 259)
This is the most attractive vase in the Hermitage's collection of Hispano-Moorish faience. It was found in 1871, at a place called Salar near Granada, by the Spanish artist Fortuni, hence the name. The vase was intended to contain wine or water with its undecorated lower part buried in the ground. The four-legged bronze stand for the vase was also produced from Fortuni's design. The vase is covered with a glaze with a metallic iridescence (lustre) and decorated with plant ornament that passes into Arabic lettering. Its eastern opulence is a reminder that it was made in the workshops of the city of Malaga, which in the fourteenth century was still in the hands of the Moors who had invaded the Iberian peninsula some 600 years earlier.

Deer Hunt tapestry
15th – early 16th century
Alsace. Wool, silk and gold
thread. 77 x 87 cm
(Hall 259)
Tapestries both warmed
and decorated the walls of
mediaeval castles. The
horsewoman on a white
steed woven on this tapestry is an image of the
"beautiful lady" typical of
the courtly culture of the
Middle Ages. The deer that
she is pursuing among the
flowering plants is a symbol of fidelity in the language of courtly love.

**Reliquary with scenes from the life
of Saint Valeria.** Late 12th century
Limoges, France. Copper with champlevé
enamel and wood. Height: 19.5 cm; length:
27.7 cm; width: 11.7 cm. (Hall 259)
The masterpiece of the collection of mediaeval Limoges enamels, this casket was created on the occasion of the mystic betrothal
of the Duke of Aquitaine, later the English
King Richard the Lion-Heart, and Valeria,
the patron saint of Limoges, that took place
in 1170. Valeria, the heiress of Aquitania,
was said to have been beheaded for refusing
to marry a pagan ruler. Picking up her head,
she carried it to the altar of Saint Martial
who had brought Christianity to Limoges.

Seated Virgin and Child
First half of the 14th century. France
Ivory, colouring, gilding, bronze, glass
and pearls. Height: 22.5 cm. (Hall 259)
In the extensive collection of mediaeval
carved ivory a special place is occupied by
statuettes of the Virgin. The main centre for
their production was Paris. The Virgin of the
Gothic era was lithe and graceful. In her we
can detect natural poses precisely observed
from life and a welcoming expression. Yet
in repeating in miniature the sculptures of
a Gothic cathedral, the statuette of the Virgin also echoes the complex rhythms of
architectural forms: the elongated proportions, exaggeratedly pliant lines and a colourful smartness in the details.

Robert Campin (circa 1380–1444)
Virgin and Child at the Fireplace. 1430s
Oil on panel. 34 x 24.5 cm. (Hall 261)
The Hermitage diptych attributed to Robert Campin, who was formerly
known as "the Master of Flemalle", is one of the artist's finest works.
The right-hand panel of the pair is devoted to the boyhood of Christ.
The Virgin and Child depicted in the interior of a typical Low Countries
house. The carefully depicted details of the setting also have a hidden
symbolical meaning: the washbasin and towel, for example, point to
Mary's purity, while the sky through the window above Christ's head sug-
gests the invisible presence of God.

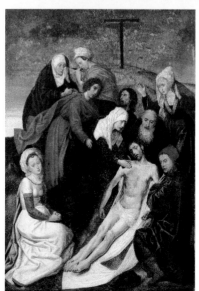

Rogier van der Weyden
(circa 1400–1464)
St Luke Painting the Virgin. 1430s
Oil on canvas, transferred from panel.
102.5 x 108.5 cm. (Hall 262)
According to legend, St Luke was an artist
and painted "from life" the first image of
the Virgin who appeared to him in
a vision with the Christ-Child in her arms.
Painters considered Luke their patron
saint and quite often gave depictions of
him features of a self-portrait, as Rogier
van der Weyden did here.

Hugo van der Goes(?) (circa 1440–1482)
The Lamentation. 1470s. Oil on panel
36.2 x 30.2 cm. (Hall 262)
Obviously a repetition, by the artist himself or a later imitator, of the right-hand
panel of a diptych that is now in the
Kunsthistorisches Museum in Vienna.

Hugo van der Goes (circa 1440–1482)
The Adoration of the Magi (triptych). 1470s
Side panels: *The Circumcision*, left
Oil on canvas, transferred from panel. 96.2 x 31.7 cm
The Massacre of the Innocents, right
Oil on canvas, transferred from panel. 96.2 x 31.7 cm. (Hall 262)
The triptych was inspired by the Gospel account of events surrounding
Christ's birth. The action begins in the depths of the left-hand panel,
which shows the meeting between Mary and Elizabeth that preceded His
birth. In the foreground there is a representation of Christ's circumcision.
The right-hand panel carries a bloody scene of the killing of the boy-
children of Bethlehem on the orders of King Herod.

Hugo van der Goes (circa 1440–1482)
The Adoration of the Magi. Central part of
the triptych. 1470s. Oil on canvas, transferred from panel. 96.3 x 77.5 cm
(Hall 262)
Following the mediaeval canons, *The Adoration of the Magi* is made up of several epi-
sodes. In the background we seen scenes of
the annunciation to the shepherds and the
meeting of the Magi on Golgotha. The

shepherds, hastening to pay reverence to
the Son of God, appear again in front of
the stable where we see bowing devoutly
before the Christ-Child three fabulous Eastern kings or the magi Balthasar, Caspar
and Melchior. This vivid, rhythmical scene
was executed in a purely Netherlandish
manner in which the careful working of
every detail is combined with an overall
monumental sense of compositional unity.

189

Jan Mandyn (active in
Antwerp in the early
16th century)
*Landscape with the Legend
of St Christopher*
Oil on panel. 71 x 98.5 cm
(Hall 262)
Mandyn was a follower of
Bosch. St Christopher is
depicted crossing a stream
carrying the Christ-Child.

Jan Provost
(circa 1465–1529)
The Virgin in Glory. 1524
Oil on canvas, transferred
from panel. 203 x 151 cm
(Hall 262)
This altarpiece is divided
into heavenly and earthly
realms. Above we see the
Virgin and Child surrounded
by a golden glow. Below,
against a landscape back-
ground, there is the biblical
King David playing on
a harp, the Roman Emperor
Augustus, sibyls (female
soothsayers) and two
prophets.

The Low Countries, 15th–16th Centuries

Gerard David
(circa 1460–1523)
Mary Embracing the Dead Christ. Late 16th century
Oil on panel. 36 x 44.5 cm
(Hall 262)
The painting was created on an oak panel, forming a single whole with the frame. In the seventeenth century, in keeping with the fashion, David's painting was set into a larger-sized board, thus acquiring a sumptuous surrounding in the form of an ornament of flower garlands.

Master of the Female Half-Lengths (the conventional designation for an unknown Netherlandish painter who probably worked in Antwerp in the 1530s and 1540s)
Female Musicians.
Oil on panel. 53 x 37.5 cm
(Hall 262)
This artist was apparently the head of a large studio that fulfilled commissions on particular themes, hence the large number of repetitions of this particular subject that exist today. The gracious images of musicians repeat one and the type of female face, embodying the ideal of beauty current in the sixteenth-century Low Countries. In some paintings in this series it is possible to read the notes of the work being performed by the girls. In the Hermitage version the music is not shown so precisely.

Dirck Jacobsz (circa 1497–1567)
Group Portrait of the Amsterdam Shooting Corporation. 1561. Oil on canvas, transferred from panel. 91 x 184.5 cm (Hall 262)
The corporations of burghers in the Low Countries were something like detachments of a reserve or militia that turned out to protect their towns and cities at moments of danger.

Frans Pourbus the Elder (1545–1581)
Portrait of a Man. 1570s. Oil on panel 87 x 78 cm. (Hall 262)
In the monumental portraits produced by Frans Pourbus we can sense the influence of artists of the Italian school, particularly Titian.

Gysbrecht Leytens (1586–after 1643)
Winter Landscape. Second quarter of the 17th century Oil on panel. 71.5 x 89 cm (Hall 258)
For a long time Leytens's works were grouped together under the conventional name "the Master of the Winter Landscapes". One of these paintings has a monogram and the mark of the Antwerp Artists' Guild on the back and that enabled researchers to determine the name of the painter.

Lucas van Leyden (1489 or 1494 – 1533)
The Healing of the Blind Man of Jericho.
Triptych. 1531. Oil on canvas,
transferred from panel. Central
composition: 115.5 x 150.5 cm;
side panels: 89 x 33.5 cm. (Hall 262)
This altar triptych was painted for a hospital
chapel in Leyden. The subject is taken from

the Gospel story, but the artist has treated
the depiction as a real-life genre scene. This
altarpiece with its bright, festive colours
and its motley crowd of people against a
landscape background is one of the artist's
finest works. The figures of heralds in the
side panels present the coats-of-arms of
those who commissioned the work.

Pieter Bruegel the Younger
(circa 1564 – 1638). *The Adoration
of the Magi.* Oil on canvas, transferred
from panel. 36 x 56 cm. (Hall 262)
The Hermitage painting is one of the many
copies that Pieter Bruegel the Younger made
of works by his father, the great sixteenth-
century Netherlandish artist Pieter Bruegel
the Elder, known as "Peasant Bruegel". The

inhabitants of a small Low Countries town
go about their everyday business as if they
had not noticed the great event unfolding
in the stable that is shifted to the left-hand
corner of the painting. The viewer, too, does
not immediately notice the figure of the
Virgin with the newly-born Christ-Child on
her lap and the group of Magi who have
come to worship the Son of God. 193

THE OLD HERMITAGE

Italy, 13th–16th Centuries

Department of Western European Art

The halls of the Old Hermitage (Halls 207–222) house the display of Italian Renaissance art (late thirteenth to sixteenth centuries), that continues in the New Hermitage (Halls 226–230). This is one of the largest collections of Italian Renaissance art outside Italy. It includes rich stocks of paintings, sculpture and applied art spanning the whole history of the Italian Renaissance from the art of the primitives at the time when Humanism was emerging in Italy (the Proto-Renaissance) to the products of Mannerism and works of the final years of the sixteenth century that are marked by the crisis of Renaissance culture. The collection is especially noted for its masterpieces by the artists of the High Renaissance.

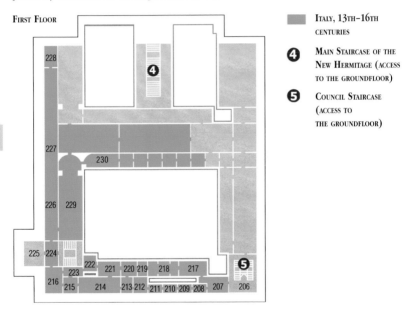

FIRST FLOOR

■ ITALY, 13TH–16TH CENTURIES

❹ MAIN STAIRCASE OF THE NEW HERMITAGE (ACCESS TO THE GROUNDFLOOR)

❺ COUNCIL STAIRCASE (ACCESS TO THE GROUNDFLOOR)

The Old Hermitage, a building adjoining the Northern Pavilion of the Small Hermitage, was constructed by the architect Yury Velten in 1771–87 to house Catherine II's art collections and library. In the early 1850s the works kept here were moved to the newly-built New Hermitage, the "Imperial Museum". It was at that time that Velten's building became known as the Old Hermitage. The rooms thus freed were redecorated by Andrei Stakenschneider who in this work used French Rococo motifs and techniques with great taste and refinement. Apartments were created here for the eldest son of Alexander II, Tsesarevich Nikolai Alexandrovich, who died, though, in 1856 without ever using them. The rooms then became the Seventh Reserve Apartments of the imperial residence (the first six were in the Winter Palace). In 1918, after the Revolution, the apartments were given over to the Hermitage and have been used for its displays ever since.

The Council Staircase. 1850–56
Architect: Andrei Stakenschneider
The Council Staircase got its name in the
nineteenth century from the adjoining
entrance that led to the premises occupied
by the State Council on the ground floor
of the Old Hermitage. The stairs were installed in place of the Oval Hall that had
housed Catherine II's library. The ceiling
painting of the Oval Hall survives, a work
by the Frenchman Gabriel François Doyen

depicting *The Virtues Presenting Youth
to the Goddess Minerva*. With great taste
the decoration of the staircase combines
artificial marble walls, Carrara marble columns, exquisite stucco work and marble
sculpture. It is made grander still by nineteenth-century works in decorative stone:
an Italian-made table with an ornament in
the form of a triumphal arch and a vase of
Urals malachite produced by the craftsmen
of the Peterhof Lapidary Works.

Niccolo di Pietro Gerini (Mentioned from 1368, died 1415). *Crucifixion with the Virgin and St John.* 1390–95 Tempera on panel. 85.5 x 52.7 cm (Hall 207)
The display of the Italian Renaissance opens with fourteenth-century works from the Proto-Renaissance when Humanism and a realistic kind of art were emerging. The founding-father of the new approach was Giotto (1267–1337) whose works cannot be found in the Hermitage. We can obtain an idea of Giotto's reforms from works by artists of his circle. Gerini, a late follower of Giotto, here combines a stylized depiction of space, denoted by the flat golden background typical of icons, with a pronounced three-dimensionality in the figures.

> **Fra Beato Angelico da Fiesole** (Circa 1400–1455). *Madonna and Child with Angels.* Circa 1425. Tempera on panel 80 x 51 cm. (Hall 209)
Fra Angelico, a Dominican monk who was one of the most poetic painters of the Early Renaissance, the Quattrocento, organically combines persuasive truth to life in the image of the Virgin with the fabulous beauty of a world in which the earthly and the divine merge in a single image of purity and tenderness.

Simone Martini (1284 ca–1344)
The Virgin from an Annunciation
Circa 1340–44. Tempera on panel
30.5 x 21.5 cm. (Hall 207)
One of the greatest representatives of the Sienese school that followed Gothic traditions, Simone Martini introduced a spirit of secular sophistication into painting. A friend of Petrarch, he worked at the papal court in Avignon, where he created a two-leaf altarpiece depicting the Annunciation. The Virgin painted on this panel of the diptych (the other side, showing the Archangel Gabriel, is in the National Gallery in Washington) is filled with grace and spirituality. The breviary in her hand seems to be an attribute of Humanist scholarship. There is a legend that the model for this painting was Laura, Petrarch's idealized beloved.

The Hall of Italian 15th-Century Sculpture. 1851–58. Architect: Andrei Stakenschneider. (Hall 210) Italian sculptors of the Quattrocento were pursuing the same goals as painters, quite often overtaking them in the search for means to depict the real world. On display in this hall are works from the famous Della Robbia studio in Florence. The main material used there was clay — unglazed in the form of terracotta or covered with coloured glazes to become majolica. The founder of the studio, Luca della Robbia (1400–1482) is represented by a terracotta bust of *The Infant John the Baptist*. Here too is a remarkable altarpiece *The Nativity* by Giovanni della Robbia (1469–1529), a joyful and colourful account set in Classical architectural forms. Close in style to the Della Robbia works is a terracotta bust by Benedetto da Maiano (1442–1497).

Studio of Andrea della Robbia 15th – early 16th century *Madonna and Child.* Majolica Height: 128 cm. (Hall 210)

Filippino Lippi (Circa 1457–1504)
The Adoration of the Christ-Child
Mid-1480s. Oil on copper, transferred
from panel. Diameter 53 cm. (Hall 213)
The son of the celebrated painter Filippo
Lippi, a renegade monk pardoned by the
Pope for his talent, and the nun with whom
he eloped, Filippino belongs to the last generation of Early Renaissance painters. This
biblical scene transfused with tenderness
and mysterious charm convincingly demon-
strates the talent of a subtle, lyrical painter.

Sandro Botticelli (1445–1510)
Saint Dominic. Early 1490s. Oil on canvas,
transferred from panel. 44.5 x 26 cm
(Hall 213)
This painting and its companion piece, *Saint
Jerome*, are the Hermitage's only late works
by Botticelli, created in the last years of the
Quattrocento. The agitated, anxious colour
scheme and gloomy atmosphere are a reflection of the disillusionment and doubts over
the correctness of Humanist ideals that came
to Botticelli at the end of his creative life.

Perugino (Pietro Vannucci) (1450–1523)
Saint Sebastian. Circa 1495. Oil on panel
53.5 x 39.5 cm. (Hall 213)
If it were not for the arrow piercing the neck of this naked youth, an attribute of St Sebastian, it would be hard to recognize the figure as the martyr who, legend has it, was shot with arrows by Roman soldiers for his adherence to Christianity. The main thing that fascinates the painter is the beauty of the young nude body, something that was first (re)discovered by the artists of the Early Renaissance.

Bernardino Fungai (1460–1516)
The Magnanimity of Scipio Africanus
Oil on panel. 62 x 166 cm. (Hall 212)
This scene from the deeds of a Roman general turned into a colourful story of Italian life with keenly observed details on one of the boards of a *cassone*. Fungai decorated a whole series of such elaborate chests.

Perugino (Pietro Vannucci) (1450–1523)
Portrait of a Young Man. Between 1495 and 1500. Oil on canvas, transferred from panel. 40.5 x 25.5 cm
The human being was the central theme of Renaissance art. This found reflection in portraiture, an art form born in the fifteenth-century. Among the first portraits is this work by Perugino. The unique appearance and character of the individual person attracted the Renaissance artist. He singled out the face, framing it with the dark patches of hat and clothing, using subtle effects of light and shade to bring about an expression of profound, thought that animates the features. This image anticipates the harmonious ideal expressed by the artists of the following generation, the age of the High Renaissance, to which Perugino's great pupil Raphael belonged.

The Leonardo da Vinci Hall. 1858–60
Architect: Andrei Stakenschneider
(Hall 214)
This grand hall of the residential apartments was created in place of the Italian
Hall of Catherine's day. Arranged around
the upper part of the walls are painted
panels by the seventeenth-century Italian
artist Padovanino. In the hall, stylized in
imitation of the French Baroque, the
architect made skilful use of coloured
stone: columns of dark grey Italian marble on pedestals of red Shoksha porphyry
with applied ornament of gilded bronze;
the Carrara marble fireplaces with lapis
lazuli and mosaic insets framed by columns of banded jasper. The doors here
are remarkable, decorated in the Boulle
technique that combines brass, tortoise-
shell and gilded bronze. On display in
this hall are two paintings by the great
Leonardo da Vinci.

Leonardo da Vinci (1452–1519)
Madonna with a Flower (The Benois Madonna). 1478. Oil on canvas, transferred from panel. 49.5 x 33 cm. (Hall 214)
This is an early work by Leonardo da Vinci in which he skilfully employs the *chiaroscuro* (modelling with light and shade) technique that he developed and achieves persuasive naturalness and warmth in the image of the Virgin. She is presented as a contemporary of the artist, with a face expressing the joy and tenderness of maternity. The flowers that she holds out to the Christ-Child evoke the movement of thought in his serious countenance, the awakening of awareness. For this reason the crucifer flower, a traditional pointer to Christ's passion, seems here to be not a Christian allusion, but a Humanist symbol of the natural world that, as Leonardo saw it, human beings were called upon to investigate.

Leonardo da Vinci (1452–1519)
The Litta Madonna. Circa 1490–91
Oil on canvas, transferred from panel
42 x 33 cm. (Hall 214)

It is believed that Leonardo began this painting while still a young man and completed it in 1490, in Milan, while in the service of Duke Lodovico il Moro. Depicting the moment of breast-feeding — a time of mysterious and intimate communion between mother and child, the artist attains a special sense of elevated peace and quiet that reigns here and child exist as one, and beyond, outside the windows, where distances fade in a tender blue haze. The Virgin's austere face, touched by translucent shadows, is illuminated by an expression of tenderness and subtle spirituality. The unity of the physical and the spiritual that makes a person truly beautiful, the harmonious ideal of the human being finds embodiment in the beautiful image of Leonardo's Madonna.

Francesco Melzi
(1493–1570). *Female Portrait, Flora*. Circa 1520
Oil on canvas. 76 x 63 cm
(Hall 215)
In this work we can sense an assured mastery of the painting techniques of Leonardo da Vinci: the type of female face, the melting shadows that bring an elusive movement to the face — the ghost of smile, the concealed gaze, the play of folds and the affectionate depiction of flowers and plants. Not without cause, Leonardo considered Francesco Melzi his favourite pupil. The idealization of the woman's image has provided grounds for considering the painting a depiction of Flora, the goddess of flowers. Quite often she is called Columbine after the flower she holds in her hand.

Correggio (Antonio Allegri) (1489/94–1534)
Female Portrait. Circa 1519
Oil on canvas. 103 x 87.5 cm
(Hall 215)
This image of a woman full of harmony and dignity is already remarkable since that portraits are rare in the work of the celebrated artist from Parma. But it is also attractive for its puzzling allusions: black clothing, the nun's hood and rope belt are signs of mourning; the laurel and ivy symbols of immortality and marital fidelity. The Greek inscription on the bowl she holds may be a quotation from Homer alluding to a draft of forgetfulness as a cure for sorrow. Perhaps this is a portrait of the poetess Ginevra Rangone who was widowed in 1517.

The Hall of Venetian Art of the 15th to early 16th centuries (Hall 217)
All the halls of the Old Hermitage overlooking the inner courtyard are occupied by Venetian Renaissance art. The collection contains works by almost all the prominent Venetian artists. In the first room (Hall 217) we find works by Jacopo Palma the Elder (1480–1528) and Cima da Conegliano (1459–1517), pupils and followers of the founder of the school, Giovanni Bellini, as well as a rare and celebrated work by Giorgione.

Giorgione (Giorgio da Castelfranco)
(Circa 1478–1510). *Judith.* Oil on canvas, transferred from panel. 144 x 66.5 cm (Hall 217)
One of the chief figures of the High Renaissance, a painter and musician closely linked to the Humanist milieu of scholars, poets and artists, Giorgione died of the plague at the age of only 32, leaving few works behind. Of his two paintings in the Hermitage, this one is world famous. Judith is an apocryphal Jewish heroine who saved her people by using her beauty and intelligence to seduce Holofernes, the enemy commander, before beheading him in his tent. The artist has not, however, depicted the instant of the deed, but a strange moment when she is left alone with the head of the defeated enemy, a moment of peace and quiet before dawn, when the first rays of the sun colour the horizon with a tender golden light and flare up in cold fire on the woman's dress. Judith stands, deep in thought, and a disturbing, mysterious link exists between her and the dead face that is frozen in a blissful smile.

Titian (Tiziano Vecellio)
(1485/90–1576). *Danaë*
Between 1546 and 1553
Oil on canvas
120 x 187 cm (Hall 221)
The great painter Titian, the
head of the Venetian school
and pride of the republic, is
represented by nine paintings in the Hermitage. The
image of Danaë, the daughter of a legendary Greek
king, condemned to solitary
celibacy by her father, but
seduced by the god Zeus,
attracted the artist's attention repeatedly. In this, one
of the four variants of the
painting, the Renaissance
artist sings the praises of
sensual, earthly beauty,
affirming the human being's
right to love and happiness.

Titian (Tiziano Vecellio)
(1485/90–1576)
Saint Sebastian. 1570s
Oil on canvas.
210 x 115.5 cm (Hall 221)
This famous masterpiece by Titian was created at the end of his long life. The painter had attained complete freedom in his command of the element of colour. He threw paints onto the canvas without preparation, allowing himself to be guided by the shift of thoughts and feelings. Out of a seemingly disorderly mass of dabs and clots of paint, the body of Sebastian is moulded glistening with a dull golden colour, full of the reflections and echoes of the gloomy lighting. He is like a Classical god, powerful, strong and well-built. With his noble forms he is set up in contrast to the disturbing, tragic chaos of the universe. The world has lost its harmony; it is almost hostile to humanity. That is how Titian's art responded to the crisis of Humanism and Renaissance ideals in the late sixteenth century. Yet the old artist retained his faith in the human being. His Sebastian is not a martyr, but a hero, a man strong in spirit, challenging the world and upholding his dignity in the struggle with it.

< **Titian (Tiziano Vecellio)** (1485/90–1576). *The Repentant Mary Magadalene.* 1560s
Oil on canvas. 119 x 97 cm (Hall 221)
Colour was the chief means, the main "language" of Titian's painting and of the Venetian school. Using a host of shades of a warm golden colour applied in rapid, translucent brushstrokes, he painted the strong young body and tear-reddened face of the Gospel sinner, shown in a moment of repentant prayer. There are glints of green in the heavy gold of the hair that has fallen around her shoulders; her clothing sparkles with colour; the horizon is tinted with molten gold. Nature in its arousal echoes the passionate agitated feeling that spiritualizes and elevates the beautiful human flesh. Thus, in his own way, sensuously and ardently, the great Venetian gave expression to the harmonious ideal of the age.

Venetian fabric. Detail (Hall 223)
"Golden Venice" was famed for its crafts. It clothed the whole of Europe in its velvets and brocades, adorned tables with luxurious glassware, and enhanced beauty with its beads and jewellery. Within the display of Venetian art visitors can see superb examples from the rich collection of Venetian fabrics, bronzes and glass.

Jug. Last quarter of the 16th century. Filigree glass. Height: 30.5 cm (Hall 223)
One of the most skilful techniques developed by Venetian glassmakers was filigree work, when a thread of white milk glass was introduced into a still hot mass of clear glass. By blowing the craftsman gave the piece the required shape and a fine filigree pattern appeared within its walls. Richness and refinement of shapes, inventiveness and astonishingly fine workmanship made Venetian glass famous. Production of glass began in Venice in the thirteenth century and was soon moved to the island of Murano. It was during the Renaissance that glassmaking reached its highest peak.

Veronese (Paolo Caliari) (1528–1588)
The Lamentation. Between 1576 and 1582
Oil on canvas. 147 x 111.5 cm (Hall 222)
Veronese — one of Titian's most brilliant
pupils, the "Bard of Venice", creator of monumental compositions that adorned the Palace of the Doges, Venetian palazzi and
churches — is represented in the Hermitage
by seven of his works. *The Lamentation* is a
masterpiece that the artist produced for the

Church of San Giovanni e Paolo in Venice.
The simple, laconic composition is stunning
in the powerful use of colour. The burning
tone in the figure of the young St John, full of
life, passion and agitation, contrasts with the
greenish hues in the dead body of Christ, that
is strong and beautiful. This is Life and Death
in their noble guise, embodied in the sacrifi-
cial act of Christ that inspires His followers
to a lofty mission.

Palma il Vecchio (Jacopo Negretti)
(1480–1528). *Portrait of a Young Man.* 1510s
Oil on canvas. 93.5 x 72 cm (Hall 218)
This is one of the masterpieces of the Early Renaissance. The new approach to art reached Venice later than Florence. Taking on board the ideals of harmony and beauty of their Florentine predecessors, the Venetians contributed to painting their innate sensuality and colourfulness. The Quattrocento purity and clarity of the image is animated in this portrait by the Venetian artist by a sense of a tense inner life. With an inherently Venetian taste for the beauty of living material he conveys the warmth of the smooth skin on the young face, the splendour of the chestnut locks, the soft velvetiness of the fabrics.

Jacopo da Pontormo (Jacopo Carucci)
(1494–1557). *Madonna and Child with Saint Joseph and John the Baptist*
1521–22. Oil on canvas
120 x 98.5 cm (Hall 216)
Pontormo was one of the main exponents of Mannerism, a tendency that arose in Florence during the Late Renaissance period. It reflected the mood of crisis and disillusionment with the Renaissance ideals that took a hold on minds under the influence of dramatic circumstances. A rejection of the principles of the harmonious ideal fostered by the High Renaissance prompted a search for one's own "manner", a means of expressing subjective feelings. The arbitrarily chosen proportions of the figures in Pontormo's painting, dissonances, agitated rhythms and sharp clashes of resonant colours evoke a disturbing, dramatic atmosphere in the image.

Antonio Rossellino (1427–1479)
Madonna and Child. Mid-15th century
Marble relief. 67 x 54 cm (Hall 212)
Employing the relief technique and deli-
cately working the marble, this outstanding
Florentine sculptor of the Early Renaissance
achieved an expressive sense of volume in
the figures of the Virgin and the Child in her
arms and an impression of the space around
them. He has brought warmth and freshness
of sensation to the cold stone, a quiet and
pure delight in the beauty of the earthly
woman and earthly world that have re-
vealed themselves to him. It is this that
makes his art imperishable, one of the symbols of the enduring value of the achievements of the Italian Renaissance.

THE HERMITAGE THEATRE

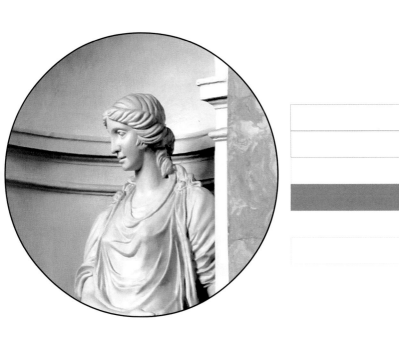

The bridge walkway to the Hermitage Theatre
1783. Architect: Yury Velten
The Hermitage Theatre was built between 1783 and 1789 to the design of Giacomo Quarenghi. He constructed the auditorium within the old Winter Palace of Peter the Great across the Winter Canal, and then erected a majestic Classical building with its main facade overlooking the Neva. A walkway raised on an arch over the Winter Canal connected the theatre with the Hermitage.

The Foyer of the Hermitage Theatre. 1783, 1902. Architects: Yury Velten; Leonty Benois. (Hall 225) The foyer of the Hermitage Theatre was created inside the covered walkway. The present decoration, in French Rococo style, dates from 1902.

**The Hermitage Theatre
The auditorium
and stage.** 1783–85
Architect: Giacomo
Quarenghi

The auditorium and stage of the Hermitage Theatre have been preserved un-changed and present a rare chance to see an eighteenth-century theatre interi-or. Quarenghi, inspired by the example of the great Italian architect Palladio, constructed the auditorium in the form of an ancient amphitheatre: rows of semicircular benches descend to a small pit area in front of the stage, where Empress Catherine had her seat. The walls of the auditorium are plastered and embellished by columns with theatrical masks on the capitals and niches con-taining statues of Apollo and the nine muses. Above the niches are medallion portraits of great dramatists. The theatre occupied a major place in court life under Catherine II. She not only loved to watch, but herself wrote plays and to part in their staging. Hermitage receptions began with theatrical performances. The theatre has been completely refurbished twice in its history, in 1894 and in 1987–89. During the latest renovation the stage was fitted with modern equip-ment. Now, as then, it serves as the setting for stage performances and concerts.

The Winter Palace of Peter the Great
A historical reconstruction

The Carriage of Peter the Great. Early 1720s(?) Elm, oak, pine, leather, velvet and metal
During the restoration of the Hermitage Theatre in 1988–89, its semi-basement was fopund to contain well-preserved elements of the old Winter Palace of Peter the Great that had been built by the architect Georg Johann Mattarnovy in the late 1710s. Part of that building had been used by Giacomo Quarenghi as a foundation when he constructed the Hermitage Theatre. After the restoration a display of the Department of Russian Culture opened here, a unique "museum within a museum" that allows visitors to view the private rooms of Tsar Peter in which he spent the last years of his life, the open gallery and inner courtyard. This carriage for short journeys was made shortly before Peter's death to designs by Nicolas Pineau.

Wax figure of Peter the Great. 1725. Carlo Bartolomeo Rastrelli (1677–174). Wax and wood. Height: 204 cm
This posthumous wax figure was created by the sculptor Carlo Bartolomeo Rastrelli at the request of Peter's widow, Catherine I. Immediately after the Emperor's death, the sculptor took a mask of his face and also made casts of his hands and feet. The final work fully reconstructed the appearance of Peter the Great. The body was made of wood, with only the hands, feet and face being of wax.

The Dining-Room in the Winter Palace of Peter the Great

The rooms in Peter's Winter Palace came down to us without their interior decoration. We do not know exactly what each was used for either. The dining-room recreated after the restoration includes an illustrative selection of objects from the Hermitage's reserve stocks that were fashionable in Peter's time. The dining table is covered with an oriental carpet, upon which are examples of silver tableware. The corked wine-bottle from the early eighteenth century was found among old builder's rubble during the restoration.

Turnery

The turnery is a recreation of Peter's beloved workshop. It contains the copying lathe on which the Tsar liked to work. By the wall is a cupboard containing turning instruments. The stove is covered with Dutch tiles that have survived in excellent condition.

THE NEW
HERMITAGE

Italy, 16th–18th Centuries
Spain, 15th–19th Centuries
Holland, 17th–18th Centuries
Flanders, 17th–18th Centuries
The Knights' Hall
The Gallery of the History of Ancient Painting

Department of Western European Art

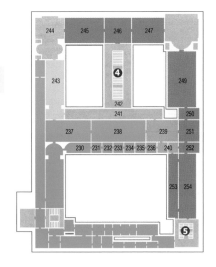

FLANDERS, 17TH–18TH CENTURIES
HOLLAND, 17TH–18TH CENTURIES
ITALY, 16TH–18TH CENTURIES
THE KNIGHTS' HALL
SPAIN, 15TH–19TH CENTURIES

4 MAIN STAIRCASE OF THE NEW HERMITAGE
(ACCESS TO THE GROUNDFLOOR)

5 COUNCIL STAIRCASE
(ACCESS TO THE GROUNDFLOOR)

In keeping with the wishes of Nicholas I, the architect Leo von Klenze created the building of the "Imperial Museum" as "part of a single whole with the palace, the dwelling of the monarch". For this reason the second-storey halls are striking for the variety and rich detail of their decoration.

The idea of opening the first public museum of art in St Petersburg came from Emperor Nicholas I. The design for the building was commissioned from the Bavarian architect Leo von Klenze who had already constructed museum buildings in Munich. The Imperial "Public Museum" was built between 1842 and 1851. The New Hermitage first formally opened its doors to visitors on 5 February 1852. The halls of ancient and modern sculpture were located on the ground floor while a white marble staircase led to the first floor and the Hermitage picture gallery. The magnificent halls in the upper storey of the New Hermitage house extremely rich stocks of Western European art from the late sixteenth century through to the eighteenth.

The Raphael Loggias (1783–92)
Architect Giacomo Quarenghi (1744–1817)
Copy of Raphael's frescoes in
the Vatican Palace (Hall 227)
The block containing the Raphael Loggias
lies alongside the Winter Canal and was
constructed by Quarenghi on Catherine II's
orders. It was later incorporated into the
New Hermitage. The original Raphael Loggias are a famous gallery in the Vatican
built in the sixteenth century by the architect Bramante and painted by Raphael and
his pupils. The copies of these frescoes
were made on canvas by the Rome-based
artist Christoph Unterberger and his as-
sistants. Thus the Hermitage acquired a
unique copy of a celebrated work of the
Italian Renaissance. Despite certain
changes in the details of the arrangement
and the dry manner in which the copies
were made, the Hermitage gallery does
give an idea of the remarkable sixteenth-
century ensemble in which the propor-
tionality and precision of the architectural
division emphasizes the decorative beauty
and expressiveness of the painting.

The Raphael Loggias
Detail of the ceiling painting (1783–92) Architect Giacomo Quarenghi (1744–1817) From the original by the architect Donato Bramante (Hall 227)
Each separate vault of the Raphael Loggias contains four pictures on biblical subjects, from the Creation and the story of Adam and Eve to the Crucifixion, harmoniously incorporated into the overall composition of the frescoes. The have become known as "Raphael's Bible".

The Raphael Loggias
(1783–92)
Detail of the wall painting Architect Giacomo Quarenghi (1744–1817) From the original by the architect Donato Bramante (Hall 227)
The gallery is made up of thirteen sections — the loggias. Its walls are covered with fanciful decorative painting featuring the grotesque ornament that Raphael created under the inspiration of the murals that he had studied in excavations of the remains of Ancient Roman buildings. Interwoven in a clear, precise rhythm are fantastic motifs formed from flowers and plants, human figures, imaginary animals, masks and playing cupids. The strict symmetry in the placement of the elements does not make the ornament rigid as even similar details are never repeated exactly.

Italy, 16th–18th Centuries

**The Raphael Hall
(Hall of 16th-Century
Italian Majolica)**
Architect Leo von Klenze
(1784–1864) (Hall 229)
This hall contains a rich
variety of remarkable
works of Italian sixteenth-
century art: in the display
cases there is a superb collection of Italian majolica;
the room is adorned by
splendid carved furniture,
while tapestries hang on
the walls. The paintings
placed on special stands
include the Hermitage's
two masterpieces by the
great Renaissance master
Raphael.

Majolica Plate. Circa 1550. Urbino, Italy
Painted tin-glazed earthenware
Diameter: 20.5 x 19 cm
The Hermitage's famous collection of Italian majolica is rich and varied: 500 works
of superb quality demonstrate a range of
styles and types of decoration. After firing
earthenware pieces were coated with
opaque glaze. A design was painted on the
glaze before a second firing. The paints
fused with the glaze to become vividly rich.

Majolica Vessel. Early 16th century
Italy. Painted tin-glazed earthenware
Height: 40 cm
Italian apothecaries began decorating their
shops with vessels painted with mythologi-
cal, literary and symbolic subject in the fifteenth century, but the finest examples of
such work date from the High Renaissance.

225

Raphael (Raffaello Santi or Sanzio) (1483–1520)
The Holy Family (Madonna and Child with the Beardless Joseph). Circa 1506. Tempera and oil on canvas, transferred from panel. 72.5 x 56.5 cm (Hall 229)

In 1504 Raphael moved from his native Umbria to Florence. There the artist became acquainted with the work of Leonardo and was noticeably influenced by it. In the calm, harmonious *Holy Family* that is transfused with a slight melancholy, the Virgin is the ideal of female beauty that Raphael created, what the artist himself described as "a certain idea" compiled from the host of beautiful faces he had seen in his life. In Raphael's work St Joseph, who at that time was customarily depicted as a bearded old man, is made to look more like some contemporary of the artist.

Raphael (Raffaello Santi or Sanzio) (1483–1520)
The Conestabile Madonna
Circa 1503. Oil on canvas, transferred from panel
17.5 x 18 cm (Hall 229)

This small-scale masterpiece that the young Raphael created before leaving Perugia is named in honour of a former owner. It bears features of the poetic style of Perugino, under whom the future great master studied. The painting was created on panel and at one time formed a single whole with the frame that was supposedly created to Raphael's design. The poor condition of the wooden base of the work, however, obliged the Hermitage's restorers to transfer the priceless painting on to canvas in 1871, as soon as it arrived from Italy.

Leo von Klenze (1784–1864). The Cabinet or Hall of Frescoes of the School of Raphael (Hall 230) The nine frescoes on subjects from the life of Venus created by pupils of Raphael come from the Villa Palatina that, according to tradition, was owned by Raphael himself. In the nineteenth century they were sold and transferred to canvas. They were already in poor condition when they came into the Hermitage in 1861, yet placed on the walls of this hall they form a splendid complement to the museum's collection of painting from the High Renaissance period.

Michelangelo (Michelangelo Buonarroti) (1475–1564). *The Crouching Boy*. Early 1530s Marble. Height: 54 cm (Hall 230) Almost all the sculptural works by this Italian genius have remained in his homeland. *The Crouching Boy* is the only work by this Renaissance giant in the Hermitage. The marble block from which the sculpture has been hewn, is not polished. The face, arms, and feet are from of fully worked. Light sliding over the rough surface of the stone intensifies the emotional, dramatic quality of the image. Such a method of execution, called "*non finito*", was typical of Michelangelo's late period.

Leo von Klenze (1784–1864)
The Small Italian Skylight Hall
(Hall 237)
The three main halls on the upper
floor of the New Hermitage are
known as skylight halls, as light en-
ters them through their glazed ceilings. They were designed for large-
sized paintings. The immense areas
of the walls are painted dark red in
imitation of the cloth that was here
originally. In keeping with Nicholas
I's wishes, all the rooms of the museum, irrespective of the nature of the
display, were given a palatial finish
befitting the imperial residence of
which they were part. Klenze produced not only the architectural
design, but also sketches for the decorative painting of the interiors,
sculptures, furniture and stands.
The collection of Italian art of the
late sixteenth to eighteenth centuries housed in the New Hermitage
is one of the finest in Europe.

Table and top. Peterhof Lapidary Works. 1850s
Barakhshan lapis lazuli. 220 x 110 cm

Tintoretto (Jacopo Robusti) (1518–1594)
The Nativity of John the Baptist. Circa 1550
Oil on canvas. 181 x 266 cm (Hall 237)
According to the Gospel, God struck Zachariah, the future father of John the Baptist, dumb for not believing that such an elderly couple as he and his wife Elizabeth could produce a child. Tintoretto, one of the greatest Venetian artists of the Late Renaissance, turns the scene into a real-life interior view of a Venetian home filled with servants and nursemaids bustling around the new-born infant and shifting towards the background the figures of the praying Zacharias and, lying in bed, Elizabeth. Mary, who is already expecting Christ, has come to visit her cousin.

Lionello Spada(?) (1576–1622)
The Martyrdom of the Apostle Peter. Late 16th century
Oil on canvas. 232 x 201 cm (Hall 237)
Lionello Spada studied under A. Carracci in Bologna and was influenced by Caravaggio. This painting was reckoned to be by Caravaggio himself when it entered the Hermitage in the late nineteenth century.

Annibale Carracci (1560–1609)
The Holy Women at the Tomb
1597–98. Oil on canvas
121 x 145.5 cm (Hall 237)
Annibale Carracci, one of the founders of the Bologna academy, is represented in the Hermitage by five works. The subject of this painting is the Gospel account of the women coming to anoint the body of Christ and to their amazement discovering the empty tomb and alongside an angel who told them the joyous news of the Resurrection.

Carlo Maratti (1625–1713)
Portrait of Pope Clement IX. 1660s
Oil on canvas. 158 x 118.5 cm
(Hall 237)
Maratti, a member of the Roman school, was influenced by Raphael and by the artists of the Bologna Academy. The Hermitage possesses eleven works by this artist, mainly paintings on religious subjects. Pope Clement IX occupied the papal throne from 1667 to 1669.

The Large Italian Skylight Hall
Archittect Leo von Klenze (Hall 238)
All the halls on the upper floor of the New
Hermitage are adorned by magnificent vases, tabletops and candelabra made of semiprecious stones. They were produced to
order by the three Russian lapidary works at
Peterhof, Yekaterinburg in the Urals and
Kolyvan in the Altai mountains. In the Large
Skylight Hall there are vases and tabletops
made of malachite by Urals craftsmen using
the Russian mosaic technique. This hall contains works of Italian art from the seventeenth and eighteenth centuries. In the
eighteenth century only one Italian school
— the Venetian — was at its height.

Giuseppe Mazzuola (1644–1725)
The Death of Adonis. 1709
Marble. Height: 193 cm (Hall 238)
The subject of this decorative Baroque statue
was derived from the ancient myth about the
handsome youth who was beloved by the
goddess Venus. When she learned that the
jealous Mars was plotting Adonis' death,
Venus tried to disuade him from going hunting, but the young man did not heed the goddess and was torn to pieces by a wild boar.
Venus' sorrow moved the gods to turn Adonis
into the flower anemone.

Luca Giordano
(1632–1705)
*The Battle between
the Lapiths and the Centaurs*
Late 17th century. Oil
on canvas. 255 x 390 cm
(Hall 238)
Giordano was a Neapolitan
who worked in almost all
the major centres of Italy.
He produced an enormous
number of paintings, earn-
ing himself the nickname
"Fa presto" (works fast).
The subject for *The Battle
between the Lapiths and the
Centaurs* comes from an-
cient myth that when the
half-men, half-horses were
invited to the wedding of
the king of the neighbour-
ing Lapiths they tried to
carry off the women. They
lost the battle and were
driven from their home-
land. The artist has used
this story to create a huge
decorative canvas filled
with the seething move-
ment of numerous figures
locked in combat.

Bernardo Bellotto (1720–1780)
Pirna from the Right Bank of the Elbe
Between 1747 and 1755. Oil on canvas
133.5 x 237.5 cm (Hall 238)
In the eighteenth century Venice produced a special type
of landscape, the *veduta* that conveyed the unique expressiveness of city scenes and, together with monumental painting, became the glory of the Venetian school.
In a *veduta* the artist not only captured the precise appearance of the buildings, but also masterfully conveyed nuances of lighting, the dynamic movement of the crowd, the
shine of the water, the colours of the sky. Bernardo Bellotto
learnt his craft from his uncle, the celebrated master of the
Venetian *veduta* Antonio Canale, known as Canaletto. At the
age of 27 Bellotto left his homeland and found fame in Germany and Poland. His paintings, especially his many depictions of Dresden and its environs, astonished contemporaries with their documentary accuracy and inventive choice
of viewpoints.

Giovanni Battista Tiepolo (1696–1770)
The Triumph of a General. Circa 1725
Oil on canvas. 546 x 322 cm (Hall 238)
Tiepolo was the best known and most celebrated Venetian artist of the eighteenth century, one of Italy's last outstanding monumental painters. The five enormous paintings in the Hermitage collection on subjects from ancient history were intended to decorate the great hall in the palace of the Venetian Dolfino family. The subjects chosen were supposed to provide the artist's contemporaries with examples of heroism, devotion to one's high civic duty and patriotism. In *The Triumph of a General,* Tiepolo has depicted the Roman commander Manius Curius Dentatus who defeated Pyrrhus, King of Epirus, and captured elephants as trophies. The artist has arranged his composition in the form of a Baroque space "open" to the viewer.

Canaletto (Antonio Canale) (1697–1768)
The Reception of the French Ambassador in Venice
1726s. Oil on canvas
181 x 229.5 cm (Hall 238)
The action in this painting unfolds against the background of St Mark's Basin. Venice, "the Queen of the Adriatic", is presented in all her splendour.

Bernardo Strozzi
(1581–1644). *The Healing of Tobit*. Cica 1635
Oil on canvas
158 x 223.5 cm (Hall 237)
The apocryphal Book of Tobit tells how the aged Tobit who had fallen blind sent his son Tobias to a distant city for some money he had left there in safekeeping. On the way Tobias was accompanied by the archangel Raphael who showed him how to restore his father's sight.

Gian Lorenzo Bernini
(1598–1680). *The Ecstasy of St Theresa*. Sketch Terracotta. Height: 47 cm (Hall 233)
Bernini, a great exponent of the Baroque style, is represented in the Hermitage by a series of *bozzetti* — terracotta sketches for famous marble works by the sculptor. *The Ecstasy of St Theresa* is a sketch for a marble group Santa Maria della Vittoria in Rome.

Caravaggio (Michelangelo Merisi dei Caravaggio) (1571–1610)
Youth with a Lute. Circa 1595
Oil on canvas. 94 x 119 cm (Hall 234)
Specialists give different interpretations of the Hermitage's only work by the great Caravaggio. Some associate it with the *vanitas* theme: merciless time will destroy the young man's beauty; the splendid flowers and fruit will wither or rot. Others hold that the objects depicted by the artist are symbols of the five senses.

Giovanni Battista Tiepolo (1696–1770). *Maecenas Presenting the Liberal Arts to Augustus*. Circa 1745
Oil on canvas
69.5 x 89 cm (Hall 235)
This work was inspired by a real historical figure, the Roman senator Gaius Cilnius Maecenas who was famous for his patronage of artists, so much so that his name came to be used for anyone who acted likewise.

**The Hall of Spanish
17th-Century Painting**
(Hall 239)
The main hall in the New
Hermitage that houses
the collection of Spanish
painting is known as
the Small Spanish
Skylight Hall.

Interest in the Spanish school of painting appeared
in Europe at the beginning of the nineteenth century,
following the Napoleonic Wars, when the works of the
greatest masters that had hitherto been kept in mon-
asteries, cathedrals and palaces began to leave the
country and appear at auctions in Paris and London.
It was then, in 1814, that the Hermitage acquired the
collection of the banker William Coesvelt who had
bought up paintings by great artists at "rock-bottom"
price in a Spain ruined by Napoleon. But as early as
Catherine II's reign Spanish works had appeared in
the Hermitage collection, mainly those by the then-
popular seventeenth-century master Murillo.
Eventually a relatively small (some 150 items), but
fairly complete collection of Spanish painting was
formed.

**Unknown Spanish Artist
of the Castilian School from
the Second Half of the 15th century**
The Deposition. Oil and tempera on panel
94 x 182 cm (Hall 240)

Luis de Morales
(between 1520 and 1525 – 1585)
*Virgin and Child with a Distaff
in the Form of a Cross.* Oil on canvas,
transferred from panel. 71.5 x 52 cm
(Hall 240)
The expressiveness and tragic exultation of
Morales's religious works are a product of
the artist's view of the world. That view was
shaped by the mysticism common in certain
Spanish circles in the sixteenth century.

< Juan Pantoja de la Cruz (1553–1608)
Portrait of Diego de Villamayor. 1605
Oil on canvas. 89 x 71 cm (Hall 240)
Pantoja de la Cruz was the court portrait-
painter to Philip II and Philip III and
worked in Madrid and the royal residence of
the Escorial. Diego de Villamayor belonged
to an aristocratic family that could trace its
roots to the eleventh century. The nobility
of the seventeen-year-old grandee is indi-
cated by the badge of the Order of Alcantara
that was granted only to a select few.

El Greco (Domenikos Theotokopoulos) (1541–1614)
The Apostles Peter and Paul Between 1587 and 1592. Oil on canvas. 121.5 x 105 cm (Hall 240)
In the sixteenth century Catholics and Protestants had different views of these two apostles. The Catholic Church exalted Peter, while the reformed confessions glorified the firmness and uncompromising position of Paul. In Catholic countries it was very rare to find a depiction of the two apostles together. The painting is apparently based on the only instance of conflict between the apostles described in the New Testament, when Paul accused Peter of inconsistency during the conversion of pagans in Antioch.

Diego Velazquez (1599–1660)
Breakfast. Circa 1617–18
Oil on canvas. 108.5 x 102 cm (Hall 239)
This early work by the great painter belongs to the *bodegon* genre. The still life
in the foreground – a pomegranate,
bread and a glass of wine — consists of
Christian symbols, while the depictions
of a boy, a young man and an old man
may have been connected with the idea
of the three periods in human life.

Diego Velazquez (1599–1660)
Portrait of the Count-Duke of Olivares
Circa 1640. Oil on canvas
67 x 54.5 cm (Hall 239)
Don Gaspar de Gusman y Pimental, Count
of Olivares, Duke of Sanlucar de Barrameda,
became a formidable prime minister from
the moment of the sixteen-year-old Philip
IV's accession to the throne. All the reins
of power came together in the hands of the
clever, cunning, educated and energetic
Olivares, whose patronage brought the
young Velazquez the post of court painter.

Francisco de Zurbaràn
(1598–1664)
St Laurence. 1636
Oil on canvas. 292 x 225 cm
(Hall 240)
According to legend Laurence, a third-century deacon of the Christian Church in Rome, was martyred by being roasted to death.
A gridiron became the usual attribute included in numerous depictions of the saint.

Francesco de Zurbaràn
(1598–1664). *Girlhood of the Virgin*. Circa 1660
Oil on canvas. 73.5 x 53.5 cm
(Hall 240)
Depicting the virgin as a young Spanish girl showing unchildlike concentration on her prayers, Zurbaràn created a work that is full of profound faith, purity and strength — qualities that mark his finest works.

Antonio Pereda (1608–1678)
Still Life. 1652. Oil on canvas. 80 x 94 cm
(Hall 240)
The still life occupied a special place in Spanish art and painters invested in it veneration for the beauty and harmonious order of objects made by human hands.

José de Ribera (1591–1652)
St Sebastian and St Irene
1628. Oil on canvas
156 x 188 cm (Hall 240)
Six paintings by Jose de Ribera open the "Golden Age" of Spanish painting in the Hermitage collection. A typical Spanish artist, sincere and religious to the point of exultation, Ribera boldly moulds form with brushstrokes of noble, restrained colours, making strong use of the *tenebroso* manner (an emphasis on darkness in contrast to light).

Francesco Goya (1746–1828)
Portrait of Antonia Sarate. Circa 1811
Oil on canvas. 71 x 58 cm (Hall 240)
Antonia Sarate was born into a well known acting family. She made her own stage debut in Madrid at the end of the eighteenth century. She was probably more celebrated among contemporaries for her beauty than her talent and if were not for two superb portraits by Goya (the second is in a private collection in Ireland) her name would probably have long since been forgotten.

Bartolome Esteban Murillo (1617–1682)
The Immaculate Conception. 1670s
Oil on canvas. 195.6 x 145 cm (Hall 240)
The Hermitage can boast over a dozen works by this celebrated master, representing various stages in his career — from the early "cold" period to the late "airy" one. *The Immaculate Conception*, painted with virtuoso skill using a bright palette of pale blue and silvery hues, is a superb example of the artist's "airy" manner.

Rembrandt Harmensz van Rijn (1606–1669) *Flora*. 1634. Oil on canvas 125 x 101 cm (Hall 254) Depicted here in the guise of Flora is Rembrandt's first wife Saskia Uylenburgh. This canvas, painted soon after their wedding, is a sort of memorial to their love. Saskia died young, in 1642.

The Hermitage's collection of paintings by the great Dutch artist Rembrandt can without exaggeration be described as unique. The more than twenty works owned by the museum (some of them perhaps created with the help of his pupils) show the complex course followed by the master over four decades of his career.

Rembrandt Harmensz van Rijn
(1606–1669). *Danaë*. 1636–42
Oil on canvas. 185 x 202.5 cm (Hall 254)
This celebrated painting was inspired by
a story popular with European artists —
the Ancient Greek myth of Princess
Danae. Her father shut her up in a tower,
condemning her to perpetual solitude, but
the god Zeus, attracted by the girl's beauty, reached her in the form of a shower
of golden rain and fathered Perseus.

Rembrandt Harmensz van Rijn
(1606–1669). *The Holy Family*. 1645
Oil on canvas. 117 x 91 cm (Hall 254)
In the 1640s, following the death of his
beloved wife, Rembrandt often turned to
the subject of the Holy Family. In the Hermitage variant light has become a spiritual as well as a physical phenomenon. Angels soar in its current. It proceeds from
a fire symbolizing the domestic hearth,
lights Jesus' cradle and Mary's face and
glows on the pages of the Bible.

243

Rembrandt Harmensz van Rijn
(1606–1669). *Descent from the Cross*. 1634
Oil on canvas. 158 x 117 cm (Hall 254)
After the Crucifixion Joseph of Arimathea
asked Pontius Pilate for the body. He, John
and other friends and followers of Jesus
removed His body from the Cross, wrapped
it and laid it in the tomb.

Rembrandt Harmensz van Rijn
(1606–1669). *Portrait of an Old Man in
Red*. 1652–54. Oil on canvas. 108 x 86 cm
(Hall 254)
The many portraits of Rembrandt's late
period were for the most part not painted
to commissions. The artist found his models among those close to him or in the
Jewish quarter of Amsterdam that was
next to his house. The old man sits immo-
bile in an armchair, immersed in his own
thoughts, his tired hands frozen in his lap.

Rembrandt Harmensz van Rijn
(1606–1669). *David and Uriah*. 1663–65
Oil on canvas. 127 x 116 cm (Hall 254)
Rembrandt's late biblical paintings are
marked by an extreme economy of expression: there is not extraneous action in
them and the setting is presented almost
without detail. Uriah here is presented
close up, walking slowly towards the viewer,
absorbed with himself. It is as if he senses
the approach of death to which he has
been condemned by King David on account
of David's love for his wife Bathsheba.
David is shown behind his back, as if already
beginning to regret the wickedness he has
committed. Profound suffering is written
on the face of the elderly scribe.

Rembrandt Harmensz van Rijn (1606–1669)
The Return of the Prodigal Son. Circa 1668–69
Oil on canvas. 262 x 205 cm
(Hall 254)
This monumental canvas is the highest manifestation of Rembrandt's mastery as a painter. The biblical parable of the prodigal son attracted many European artists. Rembrandt, who has here presented the end of the story — the return of the repentant sinner to his parents' house and his reception by his father, was probably the only one among them who in the last years of his life came to find a profound meaning in it. The painting, as immense as an altarpiece, has become an embodiment of his philosophical reflections on the chief spiritual gifts granted to human beings — the ability to love and to forgive.

245

The Tent-Roofed Hall
17th-century Dutch Art
(Hall 249)

The collection of Dutch art in the Hermitage is outstanding not only for the colossal size of the stocks (over a thousand paintings) and for the abundance of masterpieces, but also for the fact that here prominent artists are presented in the company of lesser painters whose works are in some cases rarities even in Dutch collections. This characteristic of the St Petersburg collection accurately reflects the situation that developed in middle-class Protestant Holland in the seventeenth century. No other country in Europe had such a large number of artists at that time, and nowhere else had painting become so closely bound up with people's everyday lives. The overwhelming bulk of the artists (known as "Small Dutch Masters") painted small-sized paintings to commissions from the local burghers who preferred to adorn the fairly little rooms of their houses with scenes from daily life, portraits that accurately recorded their appearance, still lifes made up of the objects around them and views of their native land.

Aert van der Neer
(1603/04–1677)
Winter View on the River
1640s. Oil on canvas
35.5 x 62 cm (Hall 249)
Van der Neer introduced
the nocturnal landscape
into Dutch art. Here he
skilfully coveys the sub-
tlest, mother-of-pearl and
pink shades of the light
on a winter's day.

Frans Hals (between 1581
and 1585 – 1666)
*Portrait of a Young Man
Holding a Glove*. Circa 1650
Oil on canvas. 80 x 66.5 cm
(Hall 249)
A brilliant master of the
portrait, using broad, virtuoso brushstrokes and disre-
garding details, Hals would
capture character in the
space of fleeting, unstable
moment. This is true of his
depiction of a young man
holding a glove.

Department of Western European Art

Jacob van Ruisdael
(1628/29–1682)
The Marsh. 1660s
Oil on canvas 72.5 x 99 cm
(Hall 249)
As a phenomenon in seventeenth-century Dutch art the work of Ruisdael can be compared in magnitude only with that of his brilliant contemporary Rembrandt. The Hermitage possesses eleven of the artist's canvases — landscapes of which the best known is this, *The Marsh*, a world-ranking masterpiece.

Gerard Ter Borch (1617–1681)
The Glass of Lemonade. 1660s
Oil on canvas, transferred from panel
67 x 54 cm (Hall 249)
Gerard Ter Borch, a remarkable colourist and keen observer of contemporary life, is represented in the Hermitage by six superb works, but the finest of them is unarguably *The Glass of Lemonade*. The artist's brush turns this scene of a procuress introducing a girl to a young soldier into a beautiful world, full of subtlety and nobility, in which refined combinations of black, grey, gold and lemon yellow hues predominate.

Willem Kalf (1619–1693)
Dessert. Second half of the 17th century. Oil on canvas
105 x 87.5 cm (Hall 249)
Dessert, a true gem by this artist, belongs to the sub-genre of the "luxurious still-life". The traditional Dutch *Breakfast* is filled out with a colourful variety of precious and exotic objects. On an expensive velvety carpet-like tablecloth the artist places a tall gilded Augsburg cup, a green glass vessel and an exquisite delicate goblet — three vertical elements that organize the composition.

Jan Steen (1626–1679)
The Revellers. Circa 1660
Oil on panel. 39 x 30 cm
(Hall 249)

The genre pieces by Jan Steen, the most witty, jolly and observant of Dutch artists, feature numerous scenes from the life of simple Dutch folk which the painter usually invested with certain ethical ideas, without, however, falling into crudity or tiresome moralizing. They could easily be interpreted by contemporaries who were able to spot the symbolic allusions and pointers in the small, everyday details that filled a composition. In this image of tipsy revellers, Steen has depicted himself and his wife, Margaretha, the daughter of the artist Jan van Goyen.

Pieter de Hooch
(1629 – after 1684)
A Woman and Her Maid
Circa 1660. Oil on canvas
53 x 42 cm. (Hall 249)

This artist managed to penetrate to the very essence of Dutch burgher life, fondly presenting its harmonious calm, clarity and purity. The bright light pouring onto the neat little Dutch courtyards, streets and people going unhurriedly about their daily tasks brings out the beauty of the most ordinary details — clothes, utensils, the brickwork of the walls, the leaves on the trees, the smooth water of a canal.

The display of Flemish art of the 17th and 18th centuries. The Snyders Hall. (Hall 245)
The Hermitage can boast one of the world's best collections of Flemish painting – more than 400 paintings by leading representatives of the school (Halls 245–248). Flemish works formed part of almost every collection purchased by Catherine II.

Flanders, one of the main regions of the southern Netherlands, underwent a powerful cultural upsurge in the seventeenth century that expressed itself most vividly in the creation of a brilliant school of painting. The independence that the Flemings achieved as a result of the revolt of the Netherlands in the late sixteenth century despite the fact that formally Flanders remained under Spanish rule fired them with enthusiasm and enhanced pride. Able to freely enjoy the wealth of the country that had been created by their own hands, the people lived with a sense of the fullness and joy of life and that transformed itself into the riot of colour and powerfully sensual forms we find in Flemish painting.

Peter Paul Rubens
(1577–1640). *Perseus and Andromeda*. Early 1620s Oil on canvas. 99.5 x 139 cm (Hall 247)
This is one of the celebrated masterpieces by Rubens, the creator and leader of the Flemish school of painting. The Classical myth rings out like a hymn of victory extolling the courage of man, the beauty of woman and the triumph of love – a hymn to life "burning with colours".

Peter Paul Rubens
(1577–1640). *The Union of Earth and Water*
Circa 1618. Oil on canvas 222.5 x 180.5 cm (Hall 247)
The union of Neptune and Cybele, the deities of sea and land, is presented as the source of life, its richness and success. The painter allegorically hinted that Flanders had to regain the mouth of the River Scheldt.

Peter Paul Rubens
(1577–1640). *Bacchus*
Between 1638 and 1640
Oil on canvas
191 x 161.3 cm (Hall 247)
This is one of Rubens's late works, a highpoint of his art. The ancient god of viniculture and wine seems to have absorbed all the colours, all the vital juices of the earth, embodying and affirming the might of the physical, sensual side of the world.

Peter Paul Rubens
(1577–1640). *Portrait of a Lady-in-Waiting to the Infanta Isabella.* Mid-1620s
Oil on panel. 64 x 48 cm
(Hall 247)
This splendid portrait is, despite the traditional title, most probably a posthumous depiction of the artist's own daughter.

Peter Paul Rubens (1577–1640)
The Descent from the Cross. Circa 1617–18
Oil on canvas. 297 x 200 cm (Hall 247)
Rubens produced this altar-piece with the aid of pupils for the church of the Capuchin Monastery in Lier, near Antwerp.

Anthony van Dyck

(1599–1641). *Family Portrait (The Family of the Landscape Painter Jan Wildens?)*. Late 1621 Oil on canvas 113.5 x 93.5 cm (Hall 246) Rubens's most gifted pupil, Anthony van Dyck became one of the greatest portraitists of the seventeenth century. He could tackle the most difficult tasks in his chosen field: from penetration into the very depths of personality in his intimate portraits to inimitable effect and grandeur in his formal likenesses. In what is believed to be a depiction of his friend and fellow painter, he used colour and precise accents of light to unite the figure of the man, woman and child in a close-knit group, a family, while creating a vivid and expressive image of each member.

Anthony van Dyck

(1599–1641). *Portrait of Elizabeth and Philadelphia Wharton*. Second half of the 1630s. Oil on canvas 162 x 130 cm (Hall 247) Van Dyck was famous for his ability to paint children. This portrait of the Wharton sisters, produced in England where he worked as "principalle Paynter in ordinary of their Majesties", would seem to fit the scheme of the formal "adult" portrait with its vertical format and elegant background. Yet the confident hand of the master conveys with a truly Flemish sense of truth – free of sentimentality and tenderness, but engaged and temperamental – the lively delight of the children's rosy faces, the enchanting roguish playfulness of the two girls pretending to be grown-up ladies.

253

Frans Snyders (1579–1657)
Fruit Shop. Oil on canvas
206 x 342 cm (Hall 245)

Frans Snyders (1579–1657). *Fishmonger's Shop*
Oil on canvas. 207 x 341 cm (Hall 245)
Pride of place in the Hermitage's collection of works by
Snyders, the creator and greatest exponent of the Flemish
still-life, goes to his *Shops*, a series of four immense canvases, each of which presents the luxurious spectacle of
the wealth and abundance of the gifts of nature. A subtle
colourist and powerful painter, Snyders produces with a
truly Flemish éclat an image of the exultant, victorious
beauty of the living world in which humanity exists,
labours and finds pleasure.

David Teniers the Younger (1610–1690)
A Peasant Wedding. 1650. Oil on canvas
82 x 108 cm (Hall 245)
A peasant wedding and other rural festivities were typical subjects for David Teniers the Younger, an outstanding Flemish master of the genre scene. The elegant colour scheme, creating an impression of festiveness, the details observed with a keen humour, and the engaging narrative presentation brought the artist success despite a certain theatrical artificiality inherent in the spectacle.

Jacob Jordaens
(1583–1678)
The Bean King. Circa 1638
Oil on canvas
157 x 211 cm (Hall 245)
This is one of the best variants of the famous painting by Jordaens, a pupil and successor of Rubens as head of the Flemish school of painting. It depicts the feast of the three kings celebrated at Epiphany. The grey-haired old man has been proclaimed the "bean king" according to custom, having found a bean in his portion of pie. The king is surrounded by members of his household excited by drink and the general merriment. The red faces, shouting mouths, stretching hands, glittering cups, children, babies and dogs – all the unrestrained, elemental nature of popular festivities is present in Jordaens's canvas.

The Knights' Hall. 1840s
Architect: Leo von Klenze. The display
of Western European arms and armour
of the 15th to 17th centuries. (Hall 243)
The collection of Western European mediaeval arms and armour contains some
5,600 items. Many were once kept in the
Tsarskoye Selo armoury. In 1885 the collection was given to the Hermitage, where
it was enlarged by new acquisitions.
The name Knights' Hall is very appropri-
ate: the majority of the display is made
up of the equipment of the mounted man
at arms: swords, crossbows and armour.

Full plate armour, introduced in the late
fourteenth century, protected both
the head and body. A suit would contain
between 60 and 160 parts, connected by
rivets and straps, and weighed between
16 and 20 kilogrammes. The separate
plates enabled the knight to move relatively easily in battle or during tourna-
ments. In the fifteenth century the form
of Gothic dress armour became fixed.
It was made precisely to measure and
came with a variety of individual details.
The mediaeval armourers of Western Europe were extremely fine craftsmen.

The cavalcade of knights
(Hall 243)

Tilt Armour. 1590
Made by Anton Peffenhauser, Augsburg, Germany. Nielloed and gilded steel
This characteristic and striking example of Gothic armour has rigid lines and slightly stretched forms. It is decorated with sumptuous plant ornament in gold on a black, nielloed background. This half suit, together with eleven other similar suits of tilting (tournament) armour, was made for Elector Christian I of Saxony.

The Gallery of the History of Ancient Painting. Architect Leo von Klenze (1784–1864) (Hall 241)
According to Klenze's concept this gallery was supposed to give visitors an idea of the development of painting and of some of the works of the great painters of ancient times that have not come down to us today. The architect selected 86 subjects and entrusted the artist Georg Hiltensperger with the creation of decorative panels to be inserted in the walls of the gallery. The paintings were executed on copper plates using wax-based paints in imitation of the ancient encaustic technique. The gallery contains a collection of sculpture by the leading exponents of Neo-Classicism at the turn of the nineteenth century Antonio Canova and Bertel Thorvaldsen.

The Gallery of the History of Ancient Painting

Antonio Canova (1757–1822)
The Three Graces. 1813. Marble
Height: 182 cm (Hall 241)
Canova created his famous *Three Graces* to a commission from Josephine Beauharnais, but the former Empress died in 1814, without ever seeing them. The work was accepted by her son, Eugène. Contemporaries were delighted by the group, believing that in it Canova had found and expressed a new ideal of beauty. It was acquired for the Hermitage collection by Nicholas I.

Vase. Mid-19th century. Malachite. (Hall 241)
The Gallery of the History of Ancient Painting is adorned by a large number of vases created by the craftsmen of the Yekaterinburg Lapidary Works using the Russian mosaic technique.

Antonio Canova (1757–1822)
Cupid and Psyche. 1796. Marble. Detail
Height: 137 cm; length: 172 cm (Hall 241)
The collection includes fifteen works by Canova. In the large group entitled *Cupid and Psyche* the sculptor has depicted an episode that shows the happy ending to the story — the god of love returns his beloved to life with a kiss. Canova has superbly connected the complex rhythms of the composition, stressing harmony and refinement in the lines of the splendid marble figures.

Antonio Canova
(1757–1822). *Hebe*
Early 19th century
Marble. Height: 158 cm
(Hall 241)
This statue of the goddess
of youth, is one of Canova's
most famous works and ex-
ists in four copies. According
to legend Hebe acted as cup-
bearer on Olympus. The
sculptor has depicted the
goddess with a jug and goblet in her hands, seemingly
sliding down a cloud on her
descent from Olympus.

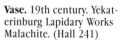

Vase. 19th century. Yekaterinburg Lapidary Works
Malachite. (Hall 241)

John Gibson (1790–1866)
Cupid the Shepherd. Marble
(Hall 241)
The English sculptor John
Gibson arrived in Rome in
1817 with a letter of recom-
mendation to Antonio
Canova in whose studio he
spent the next three years.
His works were very popu-
lar with his countrymen
and other foreign travel-
lers who enjoyed visiting
his studio in Rome and
commissioned many pieces
from him. in 1836 Gibson
was made a member of the
Royal Academy in London,
but he lived in Rome to the
end of his life.

The upper landing of the Main Staircase in the New Hermitage. Architect Leo von Klenze (1784–1864)
Twenty tall columns of grey Serdobol granite supporting the ceiling complement and complete the rhythmically elegant and chromatically refined architectural composition of the main staircase in the New Hermitage. From 1861 this area was used to display the collection of Western European sculpture of the late eighteenth and early nineteenth centuries acquired for the Imperial Museum by Nicholas I when it was still under construction. The spaces between the windows and the columns contain statues by sculptors fashionable at that time: the Italians Lorenzo Bartolini, Giovanni Dupre and Luigi Bieneme, the Germans Emil Wolff and Johann Gottfried von Schadow.
Above the two entrances to the picture gallery that are placed opposite each other are plaques commemorating the opening of the museum in both Russian and Latin: "Constructed by Emperor Nicholas I in 1852."

The Department of the Ancient World

The architect Leo von Klenze was genuinely devoted to the art of Antiquity and in his project for the New Hermitage he drew on Ancient Greek traditions. The entrance to his museum was guarded by ten granite atlantes supporting the portico. They were created in the studio of the Russian sculptor Alexander Terebenev to drawings by von Klenze.

GROUND FLOOR

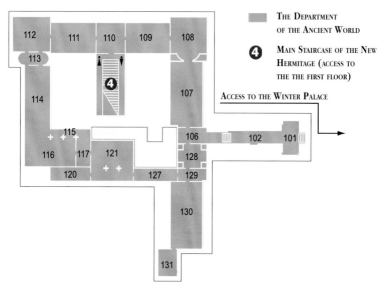

THE DEPARTMENT OF THE ANCIENT WORLD

4 MAIN STAIRCASE OF THE NEW HERMITAGE (ACCESS TO THE THE FIRST FLOOR)

ACCESS TO THE WINTER PALACE

The collections of the art of Ancient Greece and Rome, as well as artefacts found during excavations in the northern Black Sea region were installed in large, austere halls specially created for them on the ground floor of the New Hermitage. The walls of these halls, faced with stucco and artificial marble of noble shades, from red and green to pale lilac, bring out the majestic beauty of white marble statues. Rows of painted ceramic vases, glassware, metalwork and precious carved gemstones are naturally at home in the space created by the talented architect Leo von Klenze. Classical balance of proportions can also be seen in the museum fittings — the pedestals for statues, display cases, cupboards and seating for visitors were all produced in the "Neo-Grecian" style to drawings by von Klenze. The classically strict halls — rows of columns, mighty piers and caryatids beneath the vaults, exquisite Grecian ornament in the painting of the walls and ceilings, coloured marble floors – provide a worthy setting for the noble beauty of the art of the Ancient World.

Ground floor vestibule of the New Hermitage. In the foreground, *Resting Satyr.* Architect Leo von Klenze Roman copy of the original by Praxiteles First half of the 4th century B.C. Marble (Hall 110)

In 1851, in exchange for a plot of land on the Palatine Hill in Rome that belonged to the Russian imperial family, Nicholas I accepted a number of ancient statues from the Pope. These included the depiction of a resting satyr (left-hand column). A number of the works of ancient art belonging to the Hermitage collection, among them the celebrated *Taurida Venus*, had already been acquired by Peter the Great. Under Catherine II a group of ancient sculptures came into the museum from the collection of the British banker Lyde Browne, forming the core of the Hermitage stocks. The largest and most valuable assemblage of ancient sculpture came into the Hermitage in 1861 from the private museum in Rome of Giampetro Campana, Marchese di Cavelli, whose passion for collecting had bankrupted him. Thanks to him the museum acquired some 100 ancient statues and over 500 vases.

The Hall of Greek Art
of the 5th century B.C. Architect Leo von
Klenze (1784–1864) (Hall 112)
The fifth century B.C., the heyday of Classical art in Ancient Greece, is represented in
the Hermitage by statues and busts belonging to the school of the great sculptors
Myron, Phidias and Polyclitus, tomb reliefs
and red-figure vases that reflect the elevated, clear style of the high Classical period.

Euphronius (fl. 510–470 B.C.)
Psykter: *Hetaerae Feasting*. 505–500 B.C.
Painted earthenware. Height: 34 cm
Attica, Greece. (Hall 111)
This psykter, a vessel for cooling wine, is
one of the few surviving works signed by
the noted craftsman Euphronius. It bears
a depiction of *hetaerae* (courtesans) playing a game that involved pouring the last
drop of wine into an empty cup, at the
same time pronouncing words in honour
of one's beloved.

The Master of Pan. Athens
Lekythos: *Artemis and the
Swan.* 5th century B.C.
Painted earthenware
Height 38 cm (Hall 111)
The Greeks used *lekythoi* for
storing olive oil and aromatic oils. These exquisite, finely
proportioned vases were also
sometimes associated with
a funeral cult. On a white
background, quite rarely
found on such vessels, the
artist has created a strikingly
beautiful and precise depiction of Artemis, the goddess
of the hunt, feeding a swan.

Workshop of Euphronius (fl. 510–470 B.C.)
Pelike: *The Arrival of a Swallow.* Ca. 510 B.C.
Painted earthenware. Height: 37.5 cm
(Hall 111)
This red-figure wine vessel is embellished
with magnificent painting that represents the highest attainments of Ancient
Greek artists. A man, a youth and a boy
watch a swallow flying above their heads.
The inscriptions enable us to recreate
their conversation. "Look, a swallow,"
says the man. "Yes, by Hercules, a swallow," the youth exclaims. "Here it is,
spring already," the boy rejoices.

Kharinos (craftsman)
Attica. Vessel in the shape of a female head. Late 6th century B.C. Painted earthenware. (Hall 111)
Vessels of this kind are called *oenochoai*. The handle bears the artist's signature. This *oenochoe* was found in the Italian town of Vulci and is one of four that have come down to us today signed by the same craftsman.

Female statuette. Tanagra (3rd–1st century B.C.). Painted terracotta Height 18.5 cm (Hall 121)
These small, exceptionally elegant, skilfully moulded statuettes from the Hellenistic era are remarkable examples of the ancient art of coroplastics — sculpture and relief in terracotta. In 1884 a sensational event took place in the Hermitage: the stocks of ancient art were enhanced by 235 small masterpieces from the collection of Piotr Saburov, the Russian ambassador in Athens. In Ancient Greece such statuettes were used as ornaments in the home as well as gifts to the gods.

Lekythos in the shape of a sphinx. Attica
4th century B.C. Painted earthenware, gilded
Height: 21.5 cm (Hall 118)
This vessel used for aromatic substances found in a woman's grave at Phanagoria (on the Taman peninsula, next to the Crimea) is an outstanding example of Greek pottery. The Greeks borrowed the image of the sphinx from Egypt, but the Greek sphinx looks like a beautiful golden-haired, blue-eyed creature. A gold diadem on her head and three strands of pearls at her neck complete the appearance, full of earthly feminine charm, of this mysterious character of ancient legends. The surviving colouring of the vessels enables us to judge how Greek marble statues must originally have looked when they were painted.

Cameo: *Ptolemy II and Arsinoë II* (The Gonzaga Cameo). Alexandria
3rd century B.C. Sardonyx
15.7 x 11.8 cm (Hall 121)
This masterpiece of ancient glyptics is a rare example of a large "dynastic" gem. Ptolemy II Philadelphus and his consort Arsinoë are shown in profile. The exceptional beauty of the three-layered sardonyx from which the cameo was made enabled the craftsmen to develop effects of colour — the dark lower layer serves as a background, setting off the bright, matte profiles, while the brown upper layer allowed them to carve out hair, a helmet and clothing. The cameo was presented to Alexander I by Napoleon's first wife, Josephine Beauharnais.

The Twelve-Column Hall
Architect Leo von Klenze
(Hall 130)
This hall was created especially for
the display of ancient painted
vases. Klenze had a profound
knowledge of ancient art and used
its motifs in the decoration of
the hall. It is the only example of
a museum interior from the middle
of the nineteenth century to have
retained its original appearance.

Crater: *Gigantomachy*
Lycurgus (craftsman). Apulia
4th century B.C. Painted earthenware. Height: 105 cm. (Hall 130)
This vase comes from a burial
in southern Italy that was part
of Magna Graecia. Such immense
vases, known as craters, served
as grave monuments for the local
nobility. The subject here is the
myth of the Olympian gods' struggle against the giants.

Funerary urn. Etruria
Mid-4th century
Bronze. Height: 42 cm
(Hall 130)
Etruria, a powerful country
on the Italian peninsula
with an advanced culture,
flourished in the eighth to
fifth centuries B.C. The lid
of this funerary urn is a very
rare example of bronze
sculpture. It takes the form
of a couch on which
the dead noble youth with
a neck ornament reclines
as if at a feast.

**Hydria bearing scenes
from the Eleusinian
mysteries (The Queen
of Vases).** Campagna,
4th century B.C. (Hall 130)
Painted earthenware with
reliefs. Height: 62.2 cm
This luxurious work of
ancient craftsmen, a true
"Queen of Vases", comes
from the necropolis of the
city of Cumae. On the shoulders of the vase are reliefs
depicting rituals associated
with the cult of Demeter,
the goddess of fertility.

269

The Jupiter Hall. Architect Leo von Klenze (1784–1864)(Hall 107) In the nineteenth century this hall was intended for the display of Western European sculpture, and so Klenze decorated it with bas-relief portraits of major European and Russian sculptors — Michelangelo, Thorvaldsen, Canova, Martos and Rauch. Now it houses a collection of Roman portraits, while a monumental temple sculpture has given it its name.

The Kolyvan Vase. Kolyvan Lapidary Works, Altai, Russia. 1847 Revnev jasper. Height: 2.5 m; width: 4.5 m (Hall 128) This vase is one of the finest examples of Russian lapidary (stone-cutting) art and was specially made to decorate the upper floor of the New Hermitage. Its great weight (some 19 tonnes), however, prevented it from being installed there. The craftsmen of the Altai laboured on this vase for twelve years.

Statue of Jupiter. Rome 1st century A.D. Marble and coloured plaster of Paris. Height: 347 cm (Hall 107)
This statue was found in the nineteenth century during excavation of a temple in the Rome area and derives its appearance from a lost masterpiece by Phidias, the great sculptor of the fifth century B.C. The Ancient Greek craftsman created his statue of Zeus in the chryselephantine technique, combining ivory and gold. The Hermitage statue was originally created in the acrolithic technique that combined marble with gilded wood. The wooden elements have not survived and have been replaced by coloured plaster of Paris.

Portrait of an Unknown (Syrian) Woman 2nd century A.D. Marble. Height: 25.5 cm (Hall 107)
In the second century the Roman sculptural portrait was at its height. We do not today know the names of the splendid craftsmen who reached peaks of perfection in conveying shades of character, mood and appearance in their subjects. This portrait of a lady, to whom tradition has attached the epithet Syrian, is one of the masterpieces of Roman portrait sculpture. The polish on the marble creates a sense of the thinness and smoothness of skin. The thick hair arranges in an elaborate coiffure brings out the softness in the irregular features of the narrow face. The slightly faraway look and the slightly raised corners of the lips intensify the mood of concentration and self-absorption.

**Portrait of the Roman Emperor Philip
the Arabian.** Rome. 3rd century A.D.
Marble. Height: 70 cm (Hall 107)
This portrait of the "soldier-emperor"
Philip the Arabian is another of the masterpieces in the Hermitage collection. The
Emperor, a native of Bostra, the capital of
the province of Arabia, is presented as a
strong, decisive warrior, more accustomed
to a harsh life on the move that the luxu-
ries of the palace.

Bust of Empress Salonina. Mid-3rd century A.D. Marble. Height: 57 cm (Hall 107)
Julia Cornelia Salonina, the wife of Emperor
Gallenius, is presented in the guise of Venus
the primogenatrix. Yet in this work executed in the best traditions of Roman portrait
sculpture there is no idealization. On the
contrary, the skilled sculptor conveyed the
difficult character of the Empress, a woman
no longer young, arrogant and capricious.

Portrait of the Roman Emperor Balbinus
Second quarter of the 3rd century A.D.
Marble. Height: 72.5 cm (Hall 107)
Balbinus, who managed to rule for only
a few months before being killed by his own
guards, looks tired and aged in his portrait,
as if sensing his impending doom.

The Hall of Roman Decorative Sculpture of the 1st to 2nd Centuries (The Peristyle Courtyard) (Hall 108)
This fairly small room resembles the inner courtyard of a Roman palace.

Sarcophagus. 2nd–3rd century A.D. Marble Height: 116 cm (Hall 107) Roman sarcophagi were usually embellished with reliefs that were demonstrations of the great skill of the ancient sculptors. The walls of this sarcophagus bear a scene of a wedding attended by gods as well as humans.

273

The Taurida Venus Hall
Architect Leo von Klenze (1784–1864)
(Hall 109)
Following Klenze's concept, the ground-floor halls were faced with high-quality artificial marble of various shades that was produced to a special recipe (from what was called marble cement, a mixture of cement, ground marble and dyes). Against the red background provided by the walls in the Taurida Venus Hall the marble decorative sculpture of Ancient Rome looks especially picturesque. The hall is lit by a tier of windows set in the upper part of the walls.

The Taurida Venus Hall. Detail
This hall contains examples of monumental decorative sculpture in the form of Roman copies of the first to third centuries A.D. of lost Greek originals. The gardens and parks of Ancient Rome were adorned by a host of statues of the gods, but undoubtedly the most popular were depictions of Venus, the goddess of love and beauty, and also Bacchus, the god of wine, with his retinue.

The Taurida Venus
3rd century B.C. Roman copy of a Greek original
Marble. Height: 169 cm (Hall 109)

This statue of Venus was purchased in Italy on the orders of Peter the Great who planned to adorn his Summer Gardens with authentic examples of ancient sculpture. The quality of this statue, discovered during excavations, was so high that it took several years for the Italians to agree to let it go to Russia. It became the first work of ancient art in Russia. Originally it was indeed placed in the Summer Gardens, in an open pavilion. Then it was moved to the Taurida Palace of Prince Potemkin which is where it acquired its name. This image of Venus is among the works created from the original by the great Ancient Greek sculptor Praxiteles, who was the first to depict the goddess of love and beauty nude. The image of Venus with a body of elongated proportions and a small head on a long neck represents the ideal of female beauty in the Hellenistic period.

The Diamond Room

The collection of jeweller's works began to form back in the reign of the Hermitage's founder, Empress Catherine II. Notably she came into possession of the "treasures of the empresses" acquired by her predecessors. Catherine enlarged this inheritance with works commissioned from the leading jewellers of the age as well as purchases. One of the rooms in the Empress's apartments was set aside for keeping valuables and the imperial regalia and became known as "the Diamond Room". In Catherine's time too the Hermitage acquired its first pieces of ancient gold, while from the late 1830s archaeological investigations undertaken in the Crimea and southern Russia led a collection of Ancient Greek and Scythian jewellery forming in the Hermitage. Throughout the whole of the museum's history this collection has grown. At the present time the Hermitage can boast extremely rich stocks of jewellers' works from the earliest Bronze Age examples to works made by Russian and Western European masters at the beginning of the twentieth century. This collection is kept in the Golden* and Diamond Room.* The Diamond Room is located on the ground floor of the New Hermitage.

Processional cross of Saint Trudpert, the "Freiburg Cross". Second half of the 13th century. Silver and gold, champleve enamel, gilding, semiprecious and precious stones. Height: 71.5 cm
This five-ended cross carried in ceremonial processions is decorated with a fine pattern of chased ornament, a gold figure of the crucified Christ, silver ones of the Virgin, St John and, on the tips of the arms, allegorical figures of the Church triumphant and the Synagogue defeated. The cross was kept in the Monastery of St Trudpert, near Freiburg in Breisgau (SW Germany). Experts detect a combination of French and German mediaeval art in this masterpiece of the early Gothic.

Amphora. 4th century B.C. Chertomlyk burial mound. Chased and gilded silver. Height: 75 cm
This celebrated silver amphora, a masterpiece of Ancient Greek toreutics, was found during excavations of the Chertomlyk burial mound, in the grave of a Scythian ruler. The amphora is vivid proof of the contacts between the Scythians and the Greeks living on the northern Black Sea coast. The body of the vessel is covered with finely worked plant ornament typical of Greek art, while the shoulders of the vase bear an immaculately constructed, superbly detailed composition depicting Scythians taming horses.

Reliquary in the form of the figure of a deacon (St Stephen). Late 12th century France. Silver and wood with precious and semiprecious stones, gilding. Height: 42.5 cm
Great power and naive, yet persuasive faith come across in the image of St Stephen, deacon and first martyr of the Christian Church.

277

Device in the form of Catherine II's monogram. Second half of the 18th century. Gold and diamonds
This monogram of Catherine II worked in small diamonds is one of the devices worn by the Empress's ladies-in-waiting.

Snuffbox bearing a depiction of Catherine II's dog Lisette. 1770s(?) Johann Gottlieb Scharff, St Petersburg Gold with enamel, emeralds and diamonds. The snuffbox as a delightful trinket, a demonstration of the jeweller's art, was in great vogue at court in the eighteenth century. Empress Catherine II put together a large collection of snuffboxes that she purchased, received as gifts or commissioned from the best craftsmen. The distinguishing feature of the St Petersburg-based jeweller Scharff, whom the Empress quite often gave commissions, was particular work with tiny diamonds. In this piece he set them in an exquisite net pattern that embraces the top of the lid and forms a frame for the "portrait" of the Italian greyhound executed in enamel.

The Imperial Regalia (scale model)
1900. Carl Fabergé (1846–1920). Gold with diamonds, pearls, sapphires and spinel
This is a 1/10th-scale copy of the regalia, symbols of imperial power in Russia. It was created in the celebrated Fabergé jewellery workshop specially for the World Exhibition in Paris where it received the Grand Prix and a Large Gold Medal. Carl Fabergé was hailed as the greatest jeweller in Europe. The model reproduces the regalia created by Jeremie Pauzie for the coronation of Catherine II in 1763 — the Large Imperial Crown, adorned with diamonds and a large spinel, the gold orb, and the sceptre, topped with the Orlov Diamond, one of the largest in the world. The Small Crown of diamonds that Fabergé copied was made for Elizaveta Alexeyevna, the wife of Alexander I, and was used for the coronation of empresses ever since.

Bouquet of flowers made of precious and semiprecious stones in gold and silver settings

1740s. Jeremie Pauzie (?), St Petersburg
Gold, silver, diamonds, precious and decorative stones, glass and fabric. 13 x 19 cm
This is one of the few surviving examples of the bouquets of precious stones that were in fashion at the court of Empress Elizabeth. It probably belonged to the Empress herself.

Watch on a chain. 1740s–50s
Pierre Le Roy (1717–1785), Paris, France
Gold and silver, diamonds, rubies, glass and enamel. Diameter: 4.7 cm
Length of the chain: 18.6 cm
A watch studded with diamonds forming an elaborate Rococo pattern and a chain, or chatelaine, by which the timepiece could be attached to the belt were an essential, addition to court attire in the eighteenth century.

Cornflowers with ears of oats
Late 19th century. Carl Fabergé, St Petersburg
Gold, diamonds, enamel, rock crystal
Height: 19 cm
Pieces of enamel produced by Fabergé's workshop displayed a special style and were considered the finest of their kind.

THE GENERAL
STAFF BUILDING

"Realms of the Eagle": The Art of Empire

Pierre Bonnard and Maurice Denis: Decorative ensembles in the Hermitage collection

The left wing of the General Staff building, extending from the arch towards the River Moika, was given to the Hermitage in the 1990s and became a new branch of the museum. It houses the displays "Realms of the Eagle" devoted to *Empire*-style art, and "Pierre Bonnard and Maurice Denis. Decorative ensembles in the Hermitage collection", as well as temporary exhibitions.

The General Staff building faces the Winter Palace, framing Palace Square on the southern side with the mighty sweep of its wings, linked by the triumphal arch crowned by the Chariot of Glory. This edifice, built between 1819 and 1827 to the design of Carlo Rossi, completed the Palace Square ensemble, the main architectural ensemble in St Petersburg. The left wing of the General Staff was intended for the Ministry of Finance and the Foreign Ministry. The main, second, storey of the building overlooking the square was allotted to the residence of the Minister of Foreign Affairs (State Chancellor). The first occupant of these apartments was Count Karl Nesselrode (1780–1862). In 1856 he was succeeded by Prince Alexander Gorchakov (1798–1883), a fellow-pupil of Pushkin at the Lyceum who became an outstanding diplomat. He left the decoration of the apartments as it had been under Nesselrode and indeed Rossi's work has survived almost unaltered down to the present. These unique historical interiors with their authentic atmosphere of the *Empire* style in architecture now contain a display of the extremely rich collection of French and Russian applied art from the early decades of the nineteenth century – the time of Napoleon's Empire in France and of the brilliant victories of the Russian Empire under Alexander I. The artistic style that formed in this period under the banners of the two imperial eagles, French and Russian, is reflected in masterpieces to be seen here.

Items from the Egyptian Service. 1806–08
Sèvres factory, France; painting from drawings
by Dominique Vivant Denon. Porcelain with cobalt
and sepia overglaze painting and gilding. (Hall 2)
Europeans discovered the art of Ancient Egypt as a result
of Napoleon's Egyptian campaign. Vivant Denon accompanied the future Emperor there.

The Ballroom. 1819–27
Architect: Carlo Rossi
(Hall 7)
This hall is the most elaborate in Nesselrode's apartments. It owes its especial
Empire refinement to the
tender pale blue of the artificial marble used for the
frieze and the pilasters, and
the blue taffeta used for the
upholstery. The ceiling
painting and mirrors in gilt
frames enhance the sense of
luxury. The ballroom con-
tains a display of works by
the celebrated Parisian master of decorative bronze
Pierre-Philippe Thomire
(1751–1843): thirteen *surtout de tables* — table cen-
trepieces, each made up of a
tray, candelabra, statuettes,
vases and other objects.

283

A large table decoration: a shallow bowl raised on a column decorated by three allegorical figures (spring, summer and autumn)
First quarter of the 19th century.
Pierre-Philippe Thomire, Paris, France.
Gilded bronze. 82 x 38 cm. (Hall 7)
This bowl raised on a column encircled by allegorical figures forms part of a large table ornament (*surtout de table*) created by Thomire and acquired by the Russian court. The court in St Petersburg was one of the master craftsman's major customers. Monumental Classical forms, the impressive weight of gilded bronze and subjects from ancient mythology — everything in Thomire's work served to affirm the might and majesty of imperial power.

Mantel Clock *The Chariot of Apollo.* Late 1790s
Pierre-Philippe Thomire, Paris, France. Gilded bronze on a red marble base. 72 x 71.6 x 23 cm (Hall 4)
This mantel clock was created in the form of a two-wheeled Roman chariot being driven by Apollo, the ancient god of the sun and patron of art. The dial is incorporated in the chariot.

The Dining-Room
1819–27. Architect: Carlo Rossi. (Hall 4)
On display in what was Count Nesselrode's dining-room, faced with light yellow artificial marble, are costumes of a cavalier of the Order of the Holy Spirit. This chivalric order was founded in the sixteenth century by King Henry III of France and revived in 1815 following the restoration of the French monarchy. The costumes belonged to Alexander I.

Decorative ensembles in the Hermitage collection

Pierre Bonnard (1867–1947)
The Mediterranean Sea. 1911. Triptych
Central panel. Oil on canvas. 407 x 152 cm
Right panel. Oil on canvas. 407 x 149 cm
Left panel. Oil on canvas. 407 x 149 cm
This triptych was commissioned by the
noted collector Ivan Morozov to decorate
the stairwell of his mansion in Moscow.
The work reflects Bonnard's impressions of
the Mediterranean resort of Saint-Tropez
where the artist spent the summer of 1909.
The following summer he returned to cre-
ate one of the finest decorative ensembles
of the early twentieth century.

Maurice Denis (1870–1943)
The Story of Psyche. 1908 The first panel
of the series "Cupid and Psyche"
Oil on canvas. 394 x 269.5 cm
Morozov commissioned a series of decorative panels, consisting of eleven paintings
and two friezes from Maurice Denis in
1907. The subject of the first panel was the
start of the love story of Cupid and Psyche:
the god first catches sight of the maiden
and is struck by her beauty.

Index of Names

Эрмитаж в кармане
Путеводитель (на английском языке)

Издательство «Альфа-Колор», Санкт-Петербург
Тел./факс (812) 326-8384 E-mail: alfac@mail.wplus.net

Printed in Finland